# THE CARLYLES AT HOME

# The Carlyles
# at Home

THEA HOLME

*Illustrated by Lynton Lamb*

*London*
OXFORD UNIVERSITY PRESS
NEW YORK   TORONTO
1965

*Oxford University Press, Amen House, London E.C.4*

GLASGOW NEW YORK TORONTO MELBOURNE WELLINGTON
BOMBAY CALCUTTA MADRAS KARACHI LAHORE DACCA
CAPE TOWN SALISBURY NAIROBI IBADAN ACCRA
KUALA LUMPUR HONG KONG

*Printed in Great Britain by*
*W. & J. Mackay & Co. Ltd., Chatham, Kent*

# FOREWORD

I SHOULD like to thank Mr. Derek Hudson for giving me the idea of writing this book; and Mr. Carew Wallace of the National Trust for permission to make use of the letters in the collection at Carlyle's House. My gratitude is also due to Mr. A. M. Woodward, grandson and executor of Kate Sterling, for permission to quote from hitherto unpublished letters of Jane and Thomas Carlyle, presented to Carlyle's House in 1962.    T.H.

# CONTENTS

CHAPTER ONE

# *The Chelsea House*

O N a June day in 1834, a hackney coach piled with luggage set
off from a lodging-house near the Gray's Inn Road to drive to
Chelsea. Inside were Thomas and Jane Carlyle, and their servant
Bessy Barnet with a bird-cage on her knee containing Jane's canary,
Chico. As the coach rumbled through Belgrave Square, Chico
burst into song, which the Carlyles hoped was a good omen.

Such reassurance was needed: in coming to London the Scots
couple had, as they put it, burnt their ships. They had a little less
than three hundred pounds on which to face the future; and
although a book about the French Revolution was in Carlyle's
mind, the chances of making money from it were thin. 'Book-
selling,' he wrote to his brother, 'is still at its lowest ebb.' He had
received gloomy impressions of the London publishing world:

'literature seems *done*, or nearly so . . . nothing seems to thrive but penny journals.' Fraser, the only publisher who gave him any encouragement, was prepared to print the projected book without cost, but could promise nothing more.

But Jane's faith in her husband's genius was unshakeable: it was she who had urged him to come to London; she was certain that there his merit as a writer must be recognized. Now that they had found a house to their liking she was ready to hurl herself enthusiastically into the business of making him a home where he could work in comfort. There had been some weeks of house-hunting and indecision; finally the die was cast in favour of Chelsea.

'Chelsea is unfashionable,' wrote Carlyle; 'it was once the resort of the Court and great however; hence numerous old houses in it, at once cheap and excellent.'

It was at the door of one of these old houses that the hackney coach drew up.

Number 5 Great Cheyne Row had been built in Queen Anne's reign when Chelsea was a fashionable resort, and it still kept its air of modest dignity. 'A right old strong roomy brick house,' Carlyle called it, adding that it was 'likely to see *three* races of their modern fashionables fall before it come down.' He rented it for £35 a year, from William Morgan of Pope's Head Alley; the agreement was for one year. He was to live there for the rest of his life.

There were eight rooms, and innumerable closets and cupboards, which appealed to Jane. The fixtures included bell-wires and cranks, an ironing board with swing legs, a twenty-three-inch copper and a large water butt in the back yard.

The solid front door with its lion's head knocker opened on to a dark and narrow panelled hall which led through an archway to the garden door, past what Carlyle described rather grandly as a 'broadish stair, with massive balustrade (in the old style) corniced and thick as one's thigh'. These hand-turned spiral banisters, and the ornamental curly carving on which they were supported, were delicate and dust-catching, and must have presented a constant challenge to generations of servants.

On each floor were two rooms, back and front, with an excrescence leading off the back one. This extra space served variously, floor by floor, as larder, china closet, dressing-room (originally, perhaps, powder closet). The house was panelled in pine—'wainscotted', as Carlyle put it, 'to the very ceiling'. Before she saw the house Jane had been anxious about this, fearing that the wainscot might harbour bugs; but she was reassured at the sight of the clean, freshly painted walls, and was soon boasting to a friend in Edinburgh of the cheapness of 'this large and comfortable tenement . . . *without bugs*'. Certainly the house looked clean: in the two ground floor rooms, which were divided by double doors, the landlord had filled in the upper part of the panelling and covered it with a pink and white flowered paper; and the panels all over the house were repainted 'almost white'.

When the party had arrived and their baggage had been dumped inside the empty house, Carlyle lit a cigar and Bessy lit the kitchen fire. Nothing could be done till Pickford arrived with the furniture, so master and mistress proceeded to eat their first meal in their London home, 'in *extempore* fashion on a box-lid covered with some accidental towel'.

Thomas Carlyle was 38, spare and long-limbed, with thin sensitive hands. An early portrait by Samuel Laurence shows him to have a thick crop of brown hair; under a wide brow, deeply set blue eyes look straight ahead, not at but through the viewer. His nose is straight and well formed, his cheeks and mouth ruddy; his lower lip and shaven jaw jut forward above a high collar and stock.

His wife, five and a half years younger, was slight, erect, quick-moving. Her six years in a remote farm-house at Craigenputtock had not diminished the elegance which was natural to her: she was impeccably neat. Her smooth black hair was parted in the centre of a high forehead; people always remembered her eyes which were large and very dark, with heavy lids and thick lashes. Her skin was inclined to be sallow, her nose tilted and her upper lip was too long; but she had good teeth and her smile must have been fascinating. 'As difficult to catch a likeness of as a flash of lightning,' the sculptor

Woolner said of Carlyle—and the description might have applied to Jane: no portrait can have done justice to that witty face.

At 2 o'clock the furniture van arrived, 'and *then*,' says Carlyle, 'began the hurly-burly.'

But after two days of picknicking, with carpenters and bell-hangers finishing their work, and pieces of furniture broken on the journey from Scotland being mended, at last the house was cleared of workmen and the floors could be swept; the carpets were laid—nailed down by Jane herself—the heavy curtains from Craigen-puttock, altered to fit the London windows, were hung on their brass rods; the books were sorted and housed, and Carlyle was settled into his library on the first floor with his writing table and one of the horsehair dining chairs, to start work as soon as he pleased. 'I sit quite snug,' he said; 'and far better than I deserve'—while his wife, recovering from the exhausting but exciting labours, wrote:

'Well! is it not very strange that I am here; sitting in my own hired house by the side of the Thames? . . . Is it not strange that I should have an everlasting sound in my ears, of men, women, children, omnibuses, carriages . . . steeple bells, door bells, gentle-man-raps, twopenny post-raps, footmen-showers-of-raps, of the whole devil to pay, as if plague, pestilence, famine, battle, murder, sudden death and wee Eppie Daidle were broken loose to make me diversion?'

Chelsea must indeed have been a contrast to Craigenputtock, where the silence was so intense that the sheep could be heard cropping the grass. London, and her new home, had an exhilarating effect: 'this stirring life,' said Jane, 'is more to my mind, and has besides a most beneficial effect on my bowels.'

Soon she was smartening up her clothes, 'making up' an old gown, turning a pelisse. Finally she went to a milliner's to buy a new bonnet, which had, she told her mother, 'an *air*. A little brown feather nods over the front of it, and the crown points like a sugar loaf!'

Carlyle was fascinated by the London streets: to wander along them, he said, was like reading 'one of the strangest everlasting

*Newspaper Columns* the eye ever opened on'. 'There is such a torrent of vehicles and faces,' he told his sister Jean, 'the slow-rolling, all-defying waggon, like a mountain in motion, the dejected Hackney-coach . . . the *distracted* Cab . . . which always some *blackguard* drives, with the fury of Jehu; the huge Omnibus . . . Butchers' and Brewers' and Bakers' Drays: all these, with wheelbarrows, trucks, dogcarts, and a nameless flood of other *sma' trash*, hold on unweariedly their ever-vexed chaotic way. And then of foot-passengers! From the King to the Beggar; all in haste, all with a look of care and endeavour; and as if there *were* really "Deevil a thing but one man oppressing another".'

He was not fond of shopping, but he was persuaded to go with Jane 'to some dim ironmonger's shop, to buy kettles and pans on the thriftiest of fair terms . . . a tinderbox with steel and flint' and a set of garden tools for six shillings.

Infected by his wife's energy, he set to work tidying up the neglected garden, where under a tangle of weeds were 'two miserable rose bushes'. Surrounded by high brick walls, the garden was secluded, and Carlyle found it 'of admirable comfort' for smoking his pipe in the evening or early morning, wandering slowly up and down in his homespun dressing-gown and a wide straw hat. He had hopes that in time something might be made to grow in the garden—'so called in the language of flattery': the London soil was poor, but two vines were established on the south wall; there was a cherry-tree, with almost ripe cherries, and a walnut-tree from which Jane harvested 'almost sixpence-worth of nuts'.

'Two old ladies on the one side, unknown character on the other' was all they knew of their neighbours. But Leigh Hunt lived round the corner, and—after sending various unpractical offers of help—became a constant visitor. He enjoyed hearing Jane playing and singing Scots ballads; and he seems also to have enjoyed the small bowl of Scots porridge to which he was invariably treated after-wards. 'Nothing in nature so interesting and delightful!' he cried as he ate up the 'excellent frugal and noble article' with a teaspoon. Jane nicknamed him the Talking Nightingale and enjoyed his pretty wit and graceful manners. Unfortunately, Mrs. Hunt's manners were not so graceful.

She was a persistent borrower, sending her servant round to beg the loan of teacups, silver spoons, glasses, porridge, tea—even, on one occasion, a brass fender, 'because the mistress happens to be out of the article'. Jane had some difficulty in getting her property back: she lost several teaspoons; 'when one sends for them the whole number can never be found'. She decided that Mrs. Hunt would soon have to be 'quite terminated with'. The Hunt *ménage*, with its wastefulness and gipsy squalor—eggshells and stale bread on the floor, wild, unkempt children whirling about among the broken chairs—filled Jane with horror. 'Is it not a shame to manage so, with eight guineas a week to keep house on!'

But it was not only Mrs. Hunt's fecklessness that Jane condemned: it was the extravagance of English housewives in general.

In one of the houses where they went to dine, she reckoned that the money spent on fruit for dessert 'would keep us in necessaries for two or three weeks'—fruit, which in her opinion was of no use but to give people the colic. Altogether, she felt thankful that she had been born on the other side of the Tweed. 'To see how they live and waste here,' she exclaimed, 'it is a wonder the whole city does not "bankrape". . . . Flinging platefuls of what they are pleased to denominate "crusts" into the ashpits!' 'In Scotland,' she adds virtuously, 'we have no such things as "crusts".'

Jane Carlyle, though she never forgot that she had been Miss Welsh of Haddington, the Doctor's daughter, waited on, looked up to as a young lady of breeding, was nevertheless extremely capable. 'She was ingenious in all works that required dexterity of hand,' Geraldine Jewsbury wrote of her; 'she could draw and paint, and she was a good carpenter.' At Craigenputtock, snowbound, she had made the bread, churned the butter, milked the cow and scrubbed the kitchen floor. And, as Miss Jewsbury said, 'she could do anything well to which she chose to give herself'.

She had chosen to give herself to be the wife of a poor man, and she was determined to make a success of it: until her husband's genius was recognized they must live as frugally as possible. Jane accepted this challenge gladly, keeping careful accounts and watching every halfpenny.

'I told Mrs. Hunt I had been very busy painting. "What?" she asked, "is it a portrait?" "Oh, no!" I told her, "something of more importance—a large wardrobe!" '

There was just enough furniture to go round, and it seemed to suit the old house, being, as Carlyle said, 'all of a strong weighty sort'. The mahogany dining chairs with their horsehair seats had belonged to Jane's father, and had been built to last. London upholsterers, impressed by their solidity, were often to ask 'Who made these chairs, ma'am?' 'In Cockneydom,' Carlyle commented cynically, 'unexampled prosperity makes another kind.'

There was a small upright piano, a few pictures and a number of books; otherwise the rooms were bare of all but essentials. Jane herself managed without a washstand till 1850, when for Christmas her husband presented her with five pounds accompanied by what he called a notekin, in which he had written, 'The Prophecy of a Washstand to the Neatest of Women. Blessings on her bonny face, and be it ever blithe to me, as it is dear blithe or not.'

In the first months at Cheyne Row Jane's face must have been blithe nearly all the time: indeed, from the tone of her letters, this may well have been the happiest period of her married life. Her health was improved; and she was stimulated by a growing circle of friends, and the certainty that her confidence in Carlyle's greatness was justified. The house was soon arranged to her satisfaction, at the lowest possible cost, and she received compliments on its appearance.

'You are like an Eve, and make a little Paradise wherever you are,' said Edward Irving on being shown into the ground floor parlour, where Jane had fitted the drawing-room carpet from Craigenputtock, filling in the corners with bits of blanket dyed to match. This double room, divided by folding doors which were always kept open, was the handsomest room in the house, with windows at each end. Jane's piano stood in the front parlour, between the fire and the window; and there was a table in each room, the back parlour being used for breakfast, as it looked east over the garden, and had the morning sun. Chico's cage stood here, on a small round table near the china closet, whence he could see the trees and sky through the window without being in a draught.

The china closet, which opened off the back parlour, was about seven feet square, and was fitted with shelves all round. In 1843, the shelves were removed and a window was put in, the only southern window in the house; in 1855 Jane bought a chiffonier to give this little room a handsome appearance. It was in this closet that, ten years later, a servant called Mary gave birth to an illegitimate child. How she came to be there is not known, but 'while she was in labour in the small room at the end of the dining-room', wrote Jane, 'Mr. Carlyle was taking tea in the dining-room with Miss Jewsbury talking to him!!! Just a thin small door between!' Miss Jewsbury took her leave, Mr. Carlyle went upstairs to read (Jane was away), and at two in the morning the new-born infant was smuggled out of the house wrapped in Mrs. Carlyle's best table napkins.

Meanwhile, in 1834, the china closet was used for storing china.

Above the front parlour was Carlyle's library, overlooking the street. The bedroom behind it was to be kept for guests; the Carlyles themselves decided to sleep on the second floor.

It is not the purpose of this book to explore the Carlyles' marital relations, which have been the subject of much controversy else- where. When they came to Cheyne Row they had been married for eight years and were childless. It was the custom for married couples to share a bed, and it is probable that in the early days at Cheyne Row they continued to sleep together in a four-poster made of mahogany and Scotch fir, with green curtains, which had been bought by Thomas in Dumfries for £6. 5s. Jane also possessed a 'red bed'—so called on account of its hangings—which had come from her home, and which she refers to as 'that bed I was born in'. This was set up in the spare bedroom. There was also a four-poster bed for Bessy, which was put into the front kitchen. Till 1865, all the Carlyles' maids slept in the basement: there was no question of their sleeping anywhere else—except when they were asked to 'air' one of the upstairs beds, when master and mistress were away.

Jane was a bad sleeper. At Cheyne Row she moved from bed to bed, from room to room, in search of sleep. Her first move was into the red bed, which was brought upstairs to the front bedroom on the second floor. There was now no spare bed, till, after her mother's death, a handsome elaborately-carved mahogany four-poster arrived from Scotland, and was set up in the first floor bedroom for the use of guests. Jane then decided to sleep in it herself, and it was carried upstairs, 'red bed' returning to the spare room. But unfortunately she now discovered that the noise in the front of the house was unbearable, and moved, with her bed, downstairs. In 1852, three feet of Jane's bedroom had to be sacrificed to enlarge the library, and the best bed would no longer fit in; so down came 'red bed' again, while the mahogany bed with its chintz hangings went upstairs, and was slept in by Emerson. This was the last move: Jane continued to sleep—and lie sleepless—in her 'own red bed' till she died.

There were two kitchens, back and front: the back kitchen, out of which opened the larder and the cavernous coal cellar, was used as a washhouse and the copper was there. There was a good-sized fire-place, which, according to the landlord, had 'swing trivets, fall down bar, sliding hobs, winder racks, and under slide'. These ingenious devices cannot have been used very often, as cooking was done in the front kitchen and it is unlikely that Jane would have used both fires. It was in this chilly stone-paved kitchen that Carlyle rigged up his shower bath, with which, as he wrote to his mother soon after their arrival, he was 'diligent', emptying bucket after bucket of cold water over himself as he stood in a tin bath below.

At least one servant, Fanny, is known to have kept her clothes in the back kitchen; but she, like the others, slept in the front kitchen, which was certainly a cosier place. Unfortunately, in the winter, the master liked to sit there in the evening, using up the fire and smoking his pipe, often till very late. One can imagine the poor girl waiting, shivering, in the washhouse, till the scrape of a chair on the flags and the sound of a pipe being knocked out

C.A.H.–B

announced that at last Mr. Carlyle was preparing to go upstairs, and she could go to bed.

The front kitchen, although below street level, had two windows through which the sun shone in the afternoon, so that at this time of day even the stone sink, fixed in the darkest corner, was faintly illuminated. In the winter, servants must have grown accustomed to working in semi-darkness. To cook a meal by the light of the fire and one candle (Jane was careful with candles, which cost tenpence a pound); to wash up without being able to see which was a stain and which the pattern on the plate; to pack away food in deep-set cupboards where it was difficult to make out what stood at the back of the shelf; to keep every corner swept clean of the stone-flagged floor, where stray crumbs attracted armies of black-beetles and mice housed in the wainscot; all this must have presented problems to the conscientious servant. To clean and be clean, in perpetual twilight, by means of pump-water and kettles, required a high degree of patience, hardihood and industry.

The kitchen range, whose fire Bessy hurried to light on arrival, was essential to the machinery of the house. Until that fire burned, no cooking could be done, no water heated. Winter and summer, day in, day out, it was lit first thing in the morning, and left to go out at night. On trivets stood the large black kettles which supplied the hot water for washing, cleaning and cooking; an iron gallows-shaped contraption in the wide chimney held a sliding hook for the stew-pot; in front of the fire hung a jack for roasting meat; at the side was the oven for baking. This first kitchen range, supplied by the landlord, was unsatisfactory; in 1852 Carlyle agreed to pay for a new one, the landlord to refund him £7. 3s. for it 'at any time the said Thomas Carlyle shall quit the said premises'. This large and efficient range came from Edinburgh, and had a boiler from which up to two gallons of hot water could be drawn from a tap. A small cistern, fixed in a nearby cupboard, was filled daily, and supplied the boiler by means of a pipe.

Meanwhile, Bessy Barnet was obliged to boil kettles. The pots and pans, begrimed with soot, were kept when not in use under the large dresser, and this compartment was suitably painted black.

Above, on the shelves, were all the dishes and plates; and there were two enormous drawers for kitchen utensils. The shallow stone sink was supplied with water by a pump, which drew upon a well under the stone floor; and this pump was still being used long after water was laid on from the waterworks, in 1852; for twelve years later Jane, arriving home, blames a servant for 'a pump-well gone irrecoverably dry'.

An oblong kitchen table of well-scrubbed deal stood in the middle of the room. It was on this table that, at Craigenputtock, Jane made her first loaf of bread. After the dough had risen she placed it in the oven and sat down to wait, feeling, she said, like Benvenuto Cellini when his cast of Perseus was thrust into the furnace. It was on this same table that, with increasing weariness, she taught a succession of servants to make 'Mr. C's sort of soup, and Mr. C's sort of puddings', when Mr. C's dyspepsia became chronic and his meals were a problem.

But in this summer of 1834 the Carlyles were both young enough and healthy enough to enjoy to the full their new home and the strange new experience of being Londoners. From their back windows they had a view, eastward through the trees, of the London sky-line dominated by Westminster Abbey and St. Paul's. From the front, by craning their necks a little, they could see the river and the Surrey hills. They enjoyed their walks in the June evenings along the bank of the Thames, watching the white-shirted cockneys in their green boats; or in the grounds of Chelsea Hospital, 'observing the old Pensioners'; or along 'a very pretty route' to Piccadilly. Carlyle marvelled at the quiet of Cheyne Row at night—'pure and silent almost as at Puttock; and the gas-light shimmer of the great Babylon hangs stretched from side to side of our horizon'.

The household was running smoothly: Bessy was an unqualified success. 'A superior sort of servant,' Jane said; while Thomas wrote to his mother, 'If she go on as we hope, and as she has begun, it will be our duty and pleasure to treat her not as a servant but as a friend.'

This halcyon state could not last: Carlyle was aware of that. 'You see all things painted here in the colours of Hope,' he wrote: 'there is no doubt but by and by we shall have them (House, Place, Servant and all) painted in the dingier colours of Reality.' It was several months before Reality prevailed. The first blow fell when Bessy Barnet gave notice: she was obliged, for family reasons, to go back to Warwickshire. Jane was faced, for the first time, with that ever-recurring nightmare, the Servant Problem.

## CHAPTER TWO

# Seven Maids

B ESSY BARNET, first of the long line of maids-of-all-work to the
Carlyles at Cheyne Row, came from Birmingham. Her mother
had been housekeeper to John Badams, a manufacturing chemist
who had invited Carlyle to his house some years before to give him a
patent cure for indigestion. The cure did not work, but Carlyle
remembered Bessy; and when he and Jane moved to London they
offered her employment. She accepted joyfully, ready, she declared,
to serve them 'anywhere under the heavenly sun'. Kindness, and to
be with those she liked, mattered more to her than wages, which
were, she assured them, the last of her thoughts. Perhaps this was
fortunate, for the wages she was offered were £8 a year.

Bessy was tall and good looking, and Carlyle told his mother that
she had 'manners and appearance... totally beyond the servant class';

while Jane was interested to discover that her servant had 'a grand-uncle in town with upwards of a hundred thousand pounds, who drives his carriage and all that; at a great dinner he had, he gave five pounds for a couple of pineapples'. She added drily that he had never given his niece a brass farthing since she came to London.

Despite a natural pride in recounting such extravagant goings-on, Bessy was a modest girl, content with her station and anxious to please. She worked with a will, cooking, scouring, washing, without complaint; then—recalled to Warwickshire by some family crisis—'our romantic maid', as Carlyle described her, parted from her employers, seemingly on the best of terms, and vanished for twenty-nine years.

In May 1863, Jane received a visit from a mysterious lady. She found her standing in the back dining-room, gazing out into the garden. The visitor was 'very tall, dressed in deep black, and when she turned round she showed me a pale beautiful face that was perfectly strange to me! But I was no stranger to her seemingly; for she glided swiftly up to me like a dream, and took my head softly between her hands and kissed my brow again and again, saying in a low dreamlike voice, "Oh, you Dear! you Dear! you Dear! Don't you know me?" I looked into her eyes in supreme bewilderment. At last light dawned on me, and I said one word—"*Bessy?*" "Yes, it is Bessy!" And then the kissing wasn't all on one side, you may fancy!'

Bessy was married, to a Dr. Blackiston—'the second son of a baronet'. Virtue had been amply rewarded, for the doctor was 'a clever energetic kind-hearted man' with an income of £2,000 a year and a 'large handsome' house at St. Leonards.

\* \* \*

'Oh, you Dear! you Dear! you Dear!' was an affectionate greeting from a servant, even after twenty-nine years. There is no doubt that Jane did inspire affection in many of the girls who worked for her. Why, then, did she find it so hard to keep a servant? In her thirty-two years at Cheyne Row, thirty-four maids came and went, not counting charwomen, little girls who had 'never been out before', and other temporary makeshifts. According to Alexander Carlyle, his aunt by marriage expected too much of her maids, and alternately spoilt them and lost her temper with them, so that in almost every case a violent scene terminated the engagement which had been entered into with such high hopes. For Jane always did have high hopes: again and again the new servant is described in glowing terms.

'She is far the most loveable servant I ever had; a gentle, pretty, sweet-looking creature, with innocent winning ways,' she wrote of one, Elizabeth Sprague, who came in 1849. 'A thoroughly bad character,' 'That dreadful Elizabeth,' she was writing a year later, when Elizabeth left in a hurry, to be followed by Emma, from Essex. 'Her manners are so *distinguished*,' wrote Jane delightedly of the newcomer, 'so self-possessed and soft-voiced, and *calm*, as only English people can be!' But after a week or two, Emma's shortcomings became all too clear. 'Mutton broth is beyond her, and in roasting, she is far from strong,' and after two months at Cheyne Row, Emma took her distinguished manners away to a new household, leaving Jane to revived hopes of her successor.

Servants were plentiful enough. In 1851 it was reckoned that one in nine females over the age of 10 went into domestic work. But the choice of a maid, to a mistress as fastidious and as sensitive as Jane Carlyle, must always have been a task of the utmost importance. Once, after interviewing several young women, she describes herself sitting 'with my elbows on the table and my head in my hands for something like half an hour praying the immortal gods to give me sound judgment'; and then consoles herself with the thought, 'but God bless me! one doesn't *marry* one's servant—one can *divorce* her in a month if one like, or in a minute paying a month's wages! so what need to take the matter so gravely?'

All the same, she did take it gravely. So much depended upon the smooth running of the household, and the training of a new servant cannot have been easy. 'She might be gone on quite comfortably with,' wrote Jane of one of these, 'in any other house but this, where it is considered a sin against the Holy Ghost to set a chair or a plate two inches off the spot they have been used to stand on! and where the servant of a week is required to know all the outs and ins of the

house as currently as the servant of ten years. Men are very un-
reasonable really and this man in particular. . . .'

As a child, Jane had caught a hissing gander by the neck and
'flung him to right about' simply by imagining herself a Roman
who aspired to a civic crown. When she was sixty she still saw herself
in the same heroic light, protecting her man of genius from the
vexations of incompetent servants.

'I have to stand between them, and imitate in a small humble way
the Roman soldier who gathered his arms full of enemies' spears and
received them all into his own breast!' 'It is this,' she adds, 'which
makes a change of servants . . . a terror to me in prospect, and an
agony in realisation—for a time!'

On engaging a new servant, Jane entered into a formal contract
with her, sealed by the presentation of a shilling—'after the good
old Scotch fashion of engagement—unknown in London—but which
I have always kept up; to the surprise and sometimes to the *terror*
of the person receiving it, who supposed it might bind her to heaven
knew what—like the shilling given to enlist a soldier!'

In Chelsea, there were two ways of finding a servant: inquiring
at the baker's shop and advertising in *The Times*. Jane was eventually
to try both; but when Bessy Barnet gave notice friends and relatives
were consulted, letters flew up and down the country, and finally a
good-natured damsel called Jane Ireland arrived from Lancaster. She
spent six months with the Carlyles, a slapdash, dreamy young
woman, who poured boiling water over Jane's foot instead of into
the coffee pot; and who was found by her master one morning at
breakfast time, sitting by the unlighted, half-scoured grate, deep in
Goethe's *Wilhelm Meister*. Carlyle, who must have been wanting
his breakfast, was impressed nevertheless, finding such unexpected
literary taste 'strange and even touching in the poor soul'. But unlit
fires and late meals and general all-round incompetence proved Jane
Ireland's undoing, and she was bundled back to Lancaster, where a
few months later she was reported to be thinking of Mrs. Carlyle
'with the greatest love and respect'. 'It is highly consolatory,' said
Jane, 'to be loved and respected by a person whom you have scolded
for six months without intermission.'

The baker's shop was now called into action, and produced a charwoman whose family were in the workhouse, and who was glad enough to be employed as stopgap till a new maid could be found. A friend, Mrs. Austin, recommended an Irish Protestant who came for a week or two, only to disappear hurriedly 'to attend a sick mother'. She was followed by an Irish Catholic, who seems to have taken offence almost at once. She went about her work grimly, with what Carlyle called 'the face of a Polar Bear'. 'An ugly woman, too,' he added.

Her reign was short. 'Our Irish Catholic housemaid proved a mutinous Irish savage,' wrote Carlyle: 'had a fixed persuasion, I could notice, that our poor house, and we, had been made for *her*, and had gone awry in the process'; and he described her bringing up the evening meal in a rage—'jingling down her plates as if they were quoits' and 'shattering the female and even the male nerves by it'. The master lost his temper, and 'in two instants more she was packing up her duds for the march, being desired "in God's name and even in the Devil's name" either to do that or conduct herself like a reasonable creature, and preferring the latter alternative'.

The Polar Bear was followed by a tiny cockney called Sarah Heather: 'Sereetha' she pronounced it, and Jane immediately nicknamed her Sereetha the Peesweep, her ineffectual lapwing-like swoops upon her work prompting the second title.

It was now August 1835, and the Carlyles had been at Cheyne Row for a year and two months. In his library, overlooking the street, Carlyle had toiled over the first volume of *The French Revolution*. The manuscript was completed in January, given to John Stuart Mill to read in February—and in March was burned to ashes by a housemaid who mistook it for waste paper. No one will ever know the true story, in which Mill's *inamorata*, Mrs. Taylor, was involved; but to Carlyle the news brought by Mill, 'pale as Hector's ghost', was a shattering blow. 'I learned last night,' he wrote to his publisher, 'that my whole First Volume . . . had been destroyed . . . and so the labour of five steadfast enough months had vanished irrecoverably; *worse* than if it had never been!'

'*That* first volume,' he said, could not be written again, 'for the spirit that animated it is past; but *another* first volume I will try.' 'Do not pity me,' he adds, 'forward me rather as a runner that tho' *tripped* down, will not lie there, but tip and run again.'

Somehow the immense effort of rewriting was made, and in September, feeling that the end was once more in sight, and 'by way of bonfire on that victorious event' (though 'bonfire' seems an odd word to choose), Carlyle decided to go to Scotland. His wife encouraged him; with the master out of the way the problem of housework would be lessened and things might be reduced to order. Carlyle, writing to his brother John, lamented 'the arrangement of that universal relation, Master and Servant, here at this time', and resolved rather recklessly 'to get some small apartment and sweep it out and arrange it for myself with my own hands rather than be bedevilled with such a set of unfortunates any more'.

But Jane ignored such flights of fancy. Her mother, Mrs. Welsh, was staying in the house, and Carlyle was sent off to Scotland with instructions to find a maidservant in Annandale.

Jane and her mother were left to the tender mercies of Sereetha.

'Now that I do not see you driven desperate with the chaos,' Jane wrote to her husband, 'I can take a quiet view of it, and even reduce it to some kind of order.'

'Mother and I,' she continues, 'have fallen naturally into a fair Division of labour, and we keep a very tidy house.'

Sereetha had not learned to cook; but, inspired perhaps by the industry of the two ladies, 'attained the unhoped-for perfection' of getting up at half past six to light the fire and lay the breakfast. Jane herself rose at seven-thirty and made the coffee. Breakfast consisted of 'bacon-ham' from Scotland, which, said Jane, 'is the life of me, making me always hungrier the more I eat of it'.

While Jane got the breakfast, Mrs. Welsh made her own bed and tidied her room; and after the meal was over she followed Sereetha down to the basement, where, said her daughter, 'she jingles and scours, and from time to time scolds Sereetha till all is right and tight there. I, above stairs, sweep the parlour, blacken the grate . . . then mount aloft to make my own bed.'

Sereetha, it is clear, could not be trusted with any but the most simple tasks: if she washed up, it was under Mrs. Welsh's direction, with a scolding for every cup or plate she chipped. But she was evidently anxious to improve, and was allowed to 'fetch up the tea-things' when company came in the evening. She was disappointed when no one came: 'were there to be no gentlemen?' she inquired when Jane asked why she had brought up cups and saucers for four.

The ladies lived simply. For dinner, 'a bit of meat roasted at the oven suffices two days cold'; supper consisted of porridge made on the parlour fire. The kitchen range was allowed to go out, for economy, when Sereetha went to bed at eight o'clock.

'The house looks very empty without you,' Jane wrote to Thomas; but her letters are full of gaiety, and she enjoyed the quiet, picnicky life with no desperate need to keep regular hours and no anxiety for Carlyle's comfort. There were jaunts by omnibus into London: She took her mother to the British Museum and was herself 'affected beyond measure' by the Elgin Marbles.

'Other sights we have seen none,' she wrote, 'except . . . the King and Queen.' Having heard from a beggar-woman that their Majesties were coming to visit the Chelsea Hospital, she hurried her mother off to see them, and 'without being kept waiting above five minutes' beheld the Royal couple 'walk past our very noses'. 'My mother's enthusiasm of loyalty on the occasion was a sight for sore eyes!' said Jane, but added, 'Poor Queen, after all! She looked so frost-bitten and anxious! curtsied, with such cowering hurried-ness, to the veriest rabble that was ever seen. I was wae to look at her . . .'*

*Queen Adelaide was unpopular at this time: many people thought her influence had been behind the King's sudden dismissal of the Whigs in the previous November. She was fiercely attacked in *The Times*: 'a foreigner is no very competent judge of English liberties, and politics are not the proper field for female enterprise'. 'I have only one desire', she is reported to have said, 'to play the part of Marie Antoinette with bravery in the coming revolution.'
But the King, by his democratic ways, endeared himself to the masses. 'Ha, old Billy, how d'ye do?' Carlyle heard little boys call out at the sight of the King driving through Hyde Park a few months before his death. 'Poor old fellow', said Carlyle, '. . . he looked fresh and decent; clear as from spring water.'

For Jane the most important event of the day was not the sight of her sovereign but the finding of a bargain. 'I came, saw, and bought—a sofa!' she writes excitedly, quickly excusing herself for the extravagance by saying that she will not need to spend much on clothes this year. Besides, the sofa would always sell again—'it is so sufficient an article'. 'So soon as you set eyes on it,' she assured her husband, 'and behold its vastness, its simple greatness, you will perceive that the thought of you was actively at work in my choice.'

The sofa was large—over six feet long—with a top and arms of carved and stained beech. It was padded and upholstered, and Jane, who had done without a sofa for so long, thought it luxurious. 'Oh, it is so soft! so easy!' she wrote to Carlyle, adding that one, or both, of them might sleep on it, should the occasion require, 'I mean for all night.' It is unlikely that the occasion ever did require, which was fortunate, as both were such bad sleepers. But the second-hand sofa, installed in the library between the window and the fire, became a permanent feature in the household. Mrs. Browning, Mrs. Macready, Miss Harriet Martineau and many other ladies, distinguished and undistinguished, were invited over the years to share its softness and easiness with their hostess; and for Jane herself it was a refuge when she was oppressed by melancholy or migraine.

Meanwhile she was too busy running up and down the house after Sereetha, and trying not to quarrel with her mother, for lying about on sofas. Mrs. Welsh was excitable and subject to moods: she had been a beautiful woman, used to getting her own way, and between her and her only child there were often clashes of temperament. She had been in 'the most gracious, bountiful mood' when Jane left Scotland in 1834, 'giving me gowns, etc'; and in 1836, when her daughter visited her at Templand, Mrs. Welsh was once again in the happiest of humours—'making a perfect fool of me with kindness,' said Jane. 'I was scarce home when she presented me with a purse she had worked me—filled with sovereigns! . . . so that I shall not be poorer for my journey.'

But now, staying in Jane's house in London, though she evidently enjoyed making herself useful, Mrs. Welsh became upset and cross.

The sudden cold weather, Jane wrote to her husband, had put her mother into a '*molto cattivo umore*'. Perhaps the ill humour was due to an upset liver, as in the same letter Mrs. Welsh is sending her love to her son-in-law and asking him to bring her one gross of pills from the chemist in Dumfries.

As well as pills, Carlyle was to bring back a servant. He wrote that he had found a girl who seemed suitable. True, she had had what they called in Annandale 'a misfortune', but Jane was not to be put off by this. 'It would be difficult,' she wrote, 'for me to say that an Annandale woman's virtue is the worse for a misfortune. I am certain that, in their circumstances, with their views and examples, I should have had one too, if not more!'

So Anne Cook was engaged, and set off with her master by steamer from Annan to Liverpool, and from there to London by 'Umpire Coach'—a journey of nearly fifty hours. 'Awkward hungry Anne,' said Carlyle, 'would hardly even eat, till bidden and directed by me.' He arrived at Holborn 'half dead', and the cab-drive to Cheyne Row, 'surrounded by luggage, and with Anne for company, seemed endless'.

Jane, in improved health and spirits, came excitedly to the door when this bedraggled party drove up. One glance at her husband showed the need for prompt action: leaving the new servant to find her way to the basement, she silently shepherded Carlyle upstairs to his library, where she thrust into his hand 'a big glass, almost a goblet, of the best sherry'. The cure worked. 'Shaved, washed, got into clean clothes, I stepped down quite new-made.'

By this time, Jane had had a look at Anne Cook.

She spoke in the broadest Scots. 'Broader Scotch,' said Carlyle, 'was never spoken or thought by any mortal in this metropolitan city.' Jane was determined to like her. 'She seems an assiduous, kindly, honest and thrifty creature; and will learn to do all I want with her quite easily.'

Soon she was being entertained by Anne's 'perfect incomprehension of everything like ceremony'. Carlyle, after his return, found it hard to sleep, and at bedtime one night Anne asked her mistress, 'If Mr. Carlyle bees ony uneasy through the nicht, and 's ga'an staiverin' aboot the hoose, will ye bid him gae us a cry at five in the morning?'

Like other maids at Cheyne Row, Anne enjoyed answering the door, and having a look at the people who came to see the Carlyles. She was fascinated by the handsome Count Pepoli, who, she told her mistress, was 'a real fine man, and nane that comes can ever be named in ae day with him'. Jane noticed that whenever Anne knew the Italian count was expected she put on 'a certain net cap with a most peculiar knot of ribbons . . . the reward of which act is an "I weesh you good day" when she lets him out'.

One day Fanny Kemble the actress 'bolted in' to see Carlyle. Jane did not take to her: 'she is Green-room all over, and with a heart all tossed up into blank verse. . . . The longer I live, the more I want naturalness in people.' On this occasion the actress was dressed in a riding habit and flourishing a whip—'but no shadow of a horse,' said Jane drily, 'only a carriage, the whip, I suppose, being to whip the cushions with, for the purpose of keeping her hand in practice'. Anne Cook opened the door to this handsome visitor but failed to announce her, being, said Jane, 'entirely in a non-plus whether she had let in "a leddy or a gentleman".'

In April 1836, Anne received a summons to return to Annan, her mother being at the point of death and unwilling to 'leave the charge of the house to any other but her dear Anne'.

Jane took a cynical view. 'One is left to conjecture,' said she, 'that the poor woman will either take the house along with her, or stay where she is till she can get it settled to her mind; in which last case it is better for all parties that my maid should stay where she is.' Anne stayed; and was still at Cheyne Row that summer, when Jane, after an illness, decided that unless she could get out of London 'she must surely die', and fled to Scotland. Carlyle was working frantically at *The French Revolution*, and was no company for a sick woman.

The flight to Scotland had an unexpected result: she came back to revel in the quiet and order of her home. 'The feeling of safety, of liberty, which came over me on re-entering my own house was really the most blessed I had felt for a great while.'

In the absence of her mistress, Anne Cook had risen to the occasion. Every grate in the house had been polished and filled 'with a supply of coloured clippings'—and 'the holes in the staircarpet all darned, so that it looks like new'. Jane was delighted with her 'best room', which looked, she said 'really inviting'. A bust of Shelley, a present from Leigh Hunt, and a Dürer print, 'handsomely framed', contributed to the improvement.

Jane brought back with her two 'scrubs' of heather, bought at her mother's back door for twopence. She hoped that the sight of Scottish heather in the Chelsea garden would be cheering to Anne. She had also 'rummaged out' the misfortune, who was referred to as 'Wee Jen', and no doubt brought news of the infant to its mother. Anne Cook was in high favour, and it looked as if Jane was really settled with a maid. Anne, for her part, developed a warm admiration for her mistress, and wondered 'where there was another lady that could stuff chair-cushions, and do anything that was needed, and be a lady too!'—which was a remark after Jane's heart.

In January 1837 Carlyle wrote the last paragraph of *The French Revolution* one evening after dinner. He was too exhausted to feel relief or exultation; but, leaving Jane reading his manuscript, walked out into the 'damp tepid kind of evening . . . up the Gloucester Road towards Kensington way'. The book had taken him nearly three years; his health was affected—'hers too by sympathy, by daily helping me with the intolerable load'. But as yet there could be no respite, for money was short, and he was engaged to give six lectures in May on German literature, which would now have to be prepared.

In May Mrs. Welsh was again staying at Cheyne Row. Carlyle was 'agitated, terrified, driven desperate' before his first lecture, which was given to an 'intelligent, partly fashionable' audience at Willis's Rooms on 1 May. So great was his relief when it was successfully over, that he gave his wife and mother-in-law each a sovereign 'to buy something with' in celebration. As soon as the six lectures were finished, he went off to Scotland, 'impatient,' he said, 'for shelter and silence. . . . One wish I had—silence! silence!'

Jane preferred to stay in London, 'having,' she wrote, 'almost a cat-like attachment to my own house'; and Mrs. Welsh stayed on to keep her company. Her mother's presence was a mixed blessing: mother and daughter were devoted to each other, but they could not live together. Carlyle blamed Mrs. Welsh. 'With literally the best intentions, (she) is a person you cannot live with peaceably on any terms I could ever discover than those of disregarding the whims, emotions, caprices, and conclusions she takes up chameleon-like by the thousand daily.'

But he left the pair together now; and, silent and melancholy in Annandale, gloomily reading *Pickwick* or 'riding down to Whinny-rigg for a plunge in the sea', did not return till, after nearly three months, his mother-in-law had gone.

No serious quarrel took place between Jane and her mother, but by the end of August Jane was alone, reading French novels, giving tea parties, and keeping enough company 'to satisfy all my social wants'. 'I have not heard from my mother,' she said, 'nor written to her yet, so I know not where she is.'

On Mrs. Welsh's third visit to Cheyne Row, in 1839, Jane's patience gave way and a scene took place which she afterwards bitterly regretted.

In March, Mrs. Welsh persuaded her daughter to give a soirée in recognition of the fact that Carlyle—by now a literary celebrity—was being invited to dinners and breakfasts, and, as he put it, 'rather rising in society'. The house was accordingly polished and furbished, and refreshments prepared on a larger scale than anything that Jane had dreamt of before: her entertainment of evening visitors had always been of the simplest. 'Tea is put down, and tiny biscuits; they sip a few drops of the tea, and one or two sugar biscuits "victuals" a dozen ordinary eaters.'

But now, as Carlyle put it, 'between twenty and thirty entirely brilliant bits of personages' were expected, and Mrs. Welsh was determined that her daughter's party should be a success. After Jane had made her preparations, her mother suddenly produced a fresh supply of delicacies that she had bought herself, together with an array of coloured candles for the table. Jane flew into a rage: such an extravagant display was ridiculous, would make her a laughing-stock, she cried as she removed dish after dish of sweetmeats. Then seizing two of the candles, she blew them out. 'They could be lit after her death,' she said, flinging them into a cupboard.

Mrs. Welsh burst into tears. Jane, shaken and remorseful, pulled herself together in time to play hostess; but the memory of the incident lingered. The soirée went off, Carlyle reported, 'in the most successful manner: at midnight I smoked a peaceful pipe, praying that it might be long before we saw the like again'.

His prayer was answered. This was the first and last soirée at Cheyne Row.

In the summer of 1837, Anne Cook had been sent back to Annan under a cloud. Was there a second 'misfortune' on the way? It seems likely. She had a 'follower'—a soldier of whom nothing is known but that he suffered from palpitations—to whom perhaps Anne's heart and virtue were lost. 'God help her,' said Jane, 'for her case is beyond the reach of mortal help.'

A 'sweet girl' called Ellen came as stopgap, and was left in charge of the house when Jane went touring with the Sterlings, 'having for the hundredth time recommended to Ellen my roses and my silver spoons—and myself to the Great Disposer of all'.

Soon after her return home a new servant arrived from Scotland. She was to stay for nearly eleven years, and deserves a chapter to herself.

CHAPTER THREE

# Kirkcaldy Helen

'S HE was one of the strangest creatures I ever saw; had an intellectual insight almost of genius, and a folly and simplicity as of infancy.'

Carlyle wrote this of Helen Mitchell, who drove up in a cab one wet blustery night in 1837. She came from Kirkcaldy, and seemed, he said, 'to have cared no more about the roar and tumult of huge London, all the way from St. Katherine's docks hither, than a clucking hen would have done, sitting safe in its hand-basket and looking unconcerned to right and left'.

Helen's story is dramatic and finally tragic; but during her ten years at Cheyne Row she was a constant source of comedy: 'her sayings and observations, her occasional criticisms on men and things' used to be retailed by Jane with appropriate actions and accent, and were, said Carlyle, 'by far the most authentic table wit I have anywhere heard'. Indeed, many of these sayings of Helen's passed into the Carlyles' private vocabulary, constituting a bond of understanding and laughter between them as long as Jane lived. Helen was small and wiry, and spoke in a broad Scots accent. She had several brothers, one of them a manufacturer of coach-fringe whose headquarters was in Dublin. He paid her short visits when business brought him to London, always inquiring if she would like him to bring her a poplin gown. He never brought it, but presumably the offer satisfied his brotherly conscience. Helen, on £12 a year, cannot have bought many gowns.

Wages had gone up at Cheyne Row; but Helen was an experienced servant; and her calm demeanour on arriving in London may have been due to the fact that she had travelled abroad. After her first outing she observed that Cheyne Walk, in her opinion, resembled the Boomjes in Rotterdam. 'Which it does,' said Carlyle. She was a great reader 'when she could snatch a bit of time'; and evidently borrowed from her employers' library. Her pithy comments on Harriet Martineau's *Maid of All Work* were repeated by Jane for the entertainment of Erasmus Darwin, who passed on the criticism to the authoress. Miss Martineau must have referred to it the next time Helen opened the door to her: Helen was overcome with confusion. 'It was a rail insipid trick in Darwin to tell Miss Martno,' she declared.

For Carlyle's writing, on the other hand, Helen had nothing but praise. 'Take care,' she was heard to say, handing over some books she had been dusting, 'that ane's the Master's Sartor Resart, and a capital thing it is—just noble in my opinion.'

Her opinion may have been influenced by the staunch loyalty she developed towards her employers, which extended to Jane's mother when she came to stay. The enthusiastic chattering energy which often grated on Jane evidently found favour with Helen. 'I declare it's no like the same hoose,' she exclaimed after Mrs. Welsh had gone; 'sae dull and dismal-like, it's just as if a corp had gaen oot!'

With Carlyle's growing fame after the publication of *The French*

*Revolution* illustrious visitors began to make their way to Cheyne Row, and answering the door was, for Helen, an adventure. Macready, Dickens, Chopin, Mazzini: famous and heroic personages appeared on the doorstep. And on 31 March 1839 'the sound of a whirlwind rushed through the street, and there stopt with a prancing of steeds and footman thunder at this door, an equipage all resplendent with skye-blue and silver, discoverable thro' blinds like a piece of the Coronation Procession, from which emanated Count d'Orsay!' The Prince of Dandies, alighting from his blue and silver coach, must have brought heads to all the windows in Cheyne Row: he was indeed a splendid sight. 'This Phoebus Apollo of Dandyism,' as Carlyle called him, was immensely tall, with flowing auburn hair. 'At first sight,' said Jane, 'his beauty seemed of that rather disgusting sort, which seems to be, like genius, "of no sex" '; but after he had gone she admitted that despite his appearance the Count was a devilish clever fellow.

Helen was deeply impressed. As soon as d'Orsay had taken his leave and the chariot with its prancing horses and pendant flunkeys had rolled away, she burst in upon her mistress, wild with excitement. If only Jane's mother had been there, she cried, if only Mrs. Welsh could have seen him—'such a most beautiful man and most beautiful carriage! The Queen's* was no show i' the world compared wi' that! Everything was so grand and so preceese.'

Not every visitor arrived in such style; nor did every visitor win from Helen such unmixed admiration. Godefroi Cavaignac was admitted by her one afternoon when Mrs. Carlyle was out. He would wait, he said, and Helen was obliged to show him into the drawing-room. Carlyle was in Scotland, and Jane was having a holiday from housekeeping; living, as she said, from hand to mouth.

'Voulez-vous me donner à diner, madame?' asked Cavaignac of Jane as soon as she appeared—'an astonishing question to a woman whose whole earthly prospects in the way of dinner were bounded there and then to one fried sole and two *pommes de terre*!' But the dark romantic *émigré*, a fugitive from the 1830 Revolution, was by

*The Carlyles watched the Coronation procession from Mrs. Basil Montagu's window; and presumably took Helen with them.

now a regular visitor at Cheyne Row; Carlyle had befriended him, and he was devoted to Jane. He could not be turned away hungry. A hurried conference with Helen produced 'a spoonful of improvised hash' to eke out the sole and potatoes; and when, as Jane said, 'this sumptuous repast was placed on the table,' the tactless man sat down to it enthusiastically, exclaiming several times *'Mon Dieu, comme j'ai faim, moi!'* His hunger can hardly have been satisfied, even at the expense of Jane's. Talking it over afterwards with Helen, she wished that there had been more to offer him. But Helen had no sympathy with gourmandizing Frenchmen. 'It's nae matter what ye gie him,' she said dourly, 'for he can aye mak the bread flee!'

Helen was solicitous about her mistress's health, inquiring anxiously during Carlyle's absence if she had no headache yet. 'And when I answer "None", she declares it to be quite mysterious.'

Jane's headaches were by now a regular feature; she was prostrated by them and took to her bed. Helen, awed and stricken, tiptoed in and out of Jane's room. 'She has no suggestiveness or voluntary help in her; but she does my bidding quietly and accurately, and when I am *very* bad, she bends over me in my bed, as if I were a little sick child, and rubs her cheek on mine! Once I found it wet with tears. One might think one's maid's tears could do little for a tearing headache; but they do comfort a little.'

Poor Helen! There is something infinitely touching in this picture of her dumb, instinctive attempt at sympathy for the mistress who, in the end, could find no sympathy for her. Helen had two great faults: she was dirty in her person and she drank. It is not certain when Helen's addiction to the bottle was first noticed, but there is a hint in September 1839 that Jane has given her a warning, which has had its effect. 'Helen goes on well hitherto, and I only pray that she may not bethink her some fine day that her "resolution deserves a dram".' It seems unlikely that much of Helen's beer money* was ever saved, however, for a year later Jane is writing to her mother-in-law, 'My poor little Helen has been gradually getting more and

---

* 'I give my Housemaid twelve pounds a year and one pound ten for *beer money* which she may drink or save—as she likes'.—J.W.C. to a prospective servant (Jessie Hiddlestone).

more into the habit of tippling, until, some fortnight ago, she rushed down into a fit of the most decided drunkenness that I ever happened to witness'.

'My poor little Helen': Jane's tone is sympathetic, though she can hardly have felt sympathetic at the time. The Carlyles were up till three in the morning, 'trying to get the maddened creature to bed'—presumably in the front kitchen. Helen had entrenched herself in a corner of the washhouse, where she crouched, '*fuffing* like a young tiger about to spring'. Nothing would induce her to move, so in the end they decided to leave her where she was: the door of this back kitchen had two stout bolts on the outside, which they fastened, afraid that if she could get out she might set fire to the house.

'Next day,' said Jane, 'she looked black with shame and despair; and the next following, overcome by her tears and promises and self-upbraidings, I forgave her again, very much to my own surprise.'

But Helen's remorse was premature. Encouraged by Jane's forgiveness, she decided to celebrate her reinstatement, and half an hour later 'was lying on the floor, dead-drunk, spread out like the three legs of Man, with a chair upset beside her, and in the midst of a perfect chaos of dirty dishes and fragments of broken crockery'.

Not only the dishes but the house must have gone dirty that day, and meals must have been a problem, for this was at ten in the morning, and for the rest of the day Helen remained on the kitchen floor, 'occasionally sitting up like a little bundle of dirt, executing a sort of whinner'. Jane, to reach the sink and food cupboards, must have had to step past this lamentable object, which seemed immovable. 'We could not imagine how she came to be so long in sobering; but it turned out she had a whole bottle of whisky hidden within reach, to which she crawled till it was finished throughout the day.'

After this Jane dismissed her—finally, as she thought. But Helen's remorse and shame were succeeded this time by utter despair. She could not face the future. 'It was all over for her on this earth, plainly, if I drove her away from me who alone have any influence with her. Beside me she would struggle—away from me, she saw no possibility of resisting what she had come to regard as her fate.'

Like a drowning woman, Helen clung desperately to her mistress; with the fatalism of the addict she knew that without Jane she was lost. In the end her pleas melted Jane's heart, and she forgave her, as she said, for the last time. 'I *could* not deny her this one more chance—the creature is so good otherwise. Since then she has abstained from drink, I believe, in every shape . . . but how long she may be strong enough to persevere in this rigid course in which lies her only hope—God knows. Meanwhile, I feel as if I had adopted a child.'

A strict régime had to be followed: all liquor was locked away, and Helen's spare time had to be supervised. Jane tried to educate her—not always an easy task. 'She is the greatest goose! but so cheery and good a goose.' There is something endearing about this goose—'the strangest mixture of philosopher and perfect idiot', Carlyle called her—entering so cheerfully and wholeheartedly into the plan for her reformation. She was taken to the National Gallery where her mistress tried to instil an interest in painting. Helen paused before a 'Virgin and Child', lost in admiration. It was indeed, she said at last, most handsome—and most expensive.

There is no suggestion that Helen ever had a follower. Perhaps her affections had been blighted by an early disappointment; certainly her opinion of the male sex seems, with the exception of her master, to have been poor, and her views on marriage cynical. John Sterling, a close friend of the Carlyles, had just lost his young wife, but Helen, clearing away the breakfast things, told Jane that he would soon marry again. 'Love nowadays,' she declared, was just 'momentary and away.' Look how quickly the woman next door had got over the death of her lover! While Mr. Brimlicombe, the milkman, had remarried only seven months after his wife's death. 'But indeed,' she added, 'I don't, for my part, think there is any love in the world nowadays like what used to long ago!' Jane, recounting this, added with relish Helen's further comment:

' "But I do think," she resumed after some interruption of dusting, "that Mr. Carlyle will be (admire the tense) a very desultory widow! He is so easily put about—and seems to take no pleasure in new females!" '

From time to time there were lapses: bottles were found, and Helen was given notice; but by now she felt herself to be an indispensable part of the Cheyne Row establishment. She refused to believe Jane serious. 'What would become of you I should just like to know—fancy you ill and me not there to take proper care of you! I think that would be a farce!' The tables were turned: Jane who had felt a responsibility for Helen as for an adopted child, now found that the child had adopted her.

She accepted the situation. After all, Helen did the best she could, and did not complain; and Jane, plagued by ill health, determined to turn a blind eye to her faults. 'My maid,' she wrote, 'continues highly inefficient, myself ditto.'

But it was not always easy to maintain this tolerant attitude. 'One morning,' wrote Jane in 1843, 'in putting down my breakfast Helen announced casually: "My! I was just standing this morning, looking up at the corner of my bed, ye ken, and there what should I see but two *bogues*! I hope there's nae mair." "You hope?" said I, immediately kindling into a fine phrenzy; "how could you live an instant without making sure? A pretty thing it will be if you have let your bed get full of bugs again!"'

Helen, adopting an aggressive innocence, produced the classic excuse that the bugs had been brought into the kitchen in a seamstress's shawl. But her mistress had been through this before. All thoughts of breakfast forgotten, she ran forthwith and tore down the bed-curtains, and 'pulled in pieces all of the bed that was pullable'. It was alive with bugs. 'Ah, mercy, mercy, my dismay was considerable!' wrote Jane, who set to energetically to deal with the situation. The house had just been cleaned and repainted, which made the discovery all the more horrifying. Helen, who still maintained that 'there was not a single bogue there' refused to take part in the dismantling and disinfecting, but 'went out of the way . . . not to be proved in the wrong', while her mistress, with the help of Pearson the builder, set about extermination.

But in spite of dirt and drink, there was a bond between mistress and maid that Jane had not the heart to break. By the following New Year's Day Helen was reinstated.

'In the morning, when I sprung out of bed half asleep,' wrote Jane, '. . . I was received into the arms of—Helen!—saluted with two hearty smacks on my two cheeks! While an immense ginger-bread cake, which she had baked more gingery than usual to suit my taste, was thrust into the breast of my nightshift. From this delicate attention you will perceive she is very good just now—and has, on the *whole*, behaved very well.'

Helen had her ups and downs: but perhaps she also had her trials. The house was tall and dusty; water and coals, brooms, brushes and slop-pails, had to be carried from the basement up three flights of stairs. Her mistress was subject to moods. And when she was in the mood for being house-proud, Jane was a maniac for cleaning—turning out rooms, washing and dyeing curtains, repaint-ing furniture, and insisting upon everything being as spotless and as highly polished as in her mother's house at Haddington.

As well as cleaning, cooking, serving and washing up the meals, Helen did all the household washing, which involved lighting a fire in the back kitchen and filling and refilling the large copper with buckets of water drawn from the pump. Hard and laborious work, which her successor considered out of the question. 'No woman living,' declared this female whose name was Isabella, 'no woman living could do the washing as well as everything else.' And when Jane retorted that one woman—Helen—had been doing it 'for the past eleven years*, "Oh yes, "she shouted hysterically, "oh yes, there *are* women that like to make slaves of themselves, and her you had was of that sort, but I will never slave myself for anybody's pleasure!" '

Helen does not seem to have regarded herself as a slave; she had a happy-go-lucky attitude to her work, and took the rough with the smooth. Her talents as a cook were limited, but seem to have sufficed for everyday needs: anything beyond the usual roasts and stews which formed the Carlyles' daily dinner found her unpre-pared. One Christmas what Jane described as 'a huge boxful of dead animals' arrived from Wales. Carlyle, whose nervous organization, according to his wife, had been worked upon by 'visions of Scrooge'

* Jane must be allowed dramatic licence: Helen had been nine years at Cheyne Row before she went to Dublin.

became 'seized with a perfect *convulsion* of hospitality, and has actually insisted on *improvising two* dinner parties with only a day between'. The improvisation of dinner parties, she continues, is all very well for the parties who have to eat them, simply, 'but for those who have to organize them and help to cook them *c'est autre chose, ma chère!*'

Helen tackled the roasting and serving of the 'dead animals' with her usual *sang-froid*; and the first dinner went off successfully. Before the second there was a crisis. 'I do not remember that I have ever sustained a moment of greater embarrassment in life,' wrote Jane, 'than yesterday when Helen suggested to me that *I* had better *stuff the turkey*—as she had *forgotten* all about it! *I* had never *known* "about it"! but as I make it a rule never to exhibit *ignorance* on *any* subject *devant les domestiques* for fear of losing their respect—I proceeded to *stuff* the turkey with the same air of calm self dependence with which I told her some time ago, when she applied to me, the whole history of the Scotch free-church dissensions—which up to this hour I have never been able to take in!'

The stuffing was a great success—'pleasanter to the taste than any stuffing I ever remember to have eaten—perhaps it was made with quite new ingredients—I do not know!' What a pity that the recipe for this ingenious stuffing was not preserved. The rest of the menu for this dinner consisted of hare soup, stewed mutton, a bread pudding and mince-pies; the hare soup had been served at the previous dinner and eked out to cover both occasions, and the same pudding course was offered to the two parties. By these expedients, Helen was spared unnecessary work; 'roasted Welsh mutton' and stewed beef which were served on the first of the two evenings, presented no serious problems, and no doubt Helen herself dined well on the remnants of these feasts.

On New Year's Day, 1844, Helen went to a party down the street. 'There were *twenty* to dine with the family,' said Jane, '(in a room the same size as ours!) and nine friends of the servants in the kitchen!'

On Helen's return Jane asked for an account of the party. ' "Oh" says she "it was just a sort of *guddle* of a thing—all eating and drinking and no fun at all".' 'A pretty good description of most dinners,' said Jane.

Helen was a small eater—accustomed to live upon left-overs: to 'scramble for a living out of ours', as Jane put it. Only once does she seem to have betrayed strong feelings about what she ate: a red herring was her one fancy—and her undoing. Helen, the easygoing Helen, flew into a rage, which manifested itself in a terrible banging and clattering of the drawing-room fire-irons, followed 'on her return to the subterranean' by a series of explosive noises from the kitchen where she was making tea. The tea tray was carried upstairs and clanked down on the mahogany flap outside the dining-room door 'as if she were minded to demolish the whole concern at one fell stroke'. As she entered the room Jane looked into her face inquiringly, 'and seeing it black as midnight . . . I said very coolly, "A little less noise, if you please; you are getting rather loud upon us". She cast up her eyes with the look of a martyr at the stake, as much as to say, "Well, if I must be quiet, I must; but you little know my wrongs". ' Jane was unable to account for this strange behaviour, but put it down to indigestion: Helen had asked that morning if she might have a red herring for her dinner—her heart had been set upon it for a long while, she had said, 'and of course so modest a petition received an unhesitating affirmative'. Now, no doubt, she was regretting that she had not eaten mutton like the rest of the household.

After tea, Geraldine Jewsbury, who was staying with the Carlyles, made her way down to the kitchen. ('She is oftener in the kitchen in one day than I am in a month,' adds Jane tartly, 'but that is irrelevant'). She had gone, apparently, in search of the cat. ' "Where is she?" she asked of Helen. "I have not seen her all night." . . .

' "The cat!" said Helen grimly, "I have all but killed her."

' "How?" said Geraldine.

' "With the besom," replied the other.

' "Why? For goodness sake?"

' "Why!" repeated Helen, bursting out into a new rage; "why indeed? Because she ate my red herring! I set it all ready on the end of the dresser, and she ran away with it, and ate every morsel to the tail—such an unheard of thing for the brute to do. Oh, if I could have got hold of her, she should not have got off with her life!"

' "And have you had no dinner?" asked Geraldine.

' "Oh, yes, I had mutton enough, but I had just set my heart on a red herring." '

'Which,' asks Jane in conclusion, 'was the most deserving of having a besom taken to her, the cat or the woman?'

But Helen, who for years had provided so much comedy, became in the end a tragic figure.

'Helen also, insignificant as she looks, has *a Destiny*!' wrote Jane in September 1846. It seemed at the time a most satisfactory destiny. Her brother, grown prosperous through large sales of coach-fringe to the railways—'with three hundred girls in his employment, a genteel house and plenty to keep it with', wrote inviting Helen to join him in Dublin as his housekeeper. The offer, as it turned out, was her undoing. But to be mistress of her brother's fine house was too good a chance to refuse. Helen, came 'with tears in her eyes and smiles on her lips' to tell her mistress that she was going to accept.

Jane was dubious. 'I wish it may end well,' she said. But she had not taken to Helen's brother—'a flustering incredible sort of man—and very selfish with the two black eyes set close together in his head'. She did not trust him: why, after all these years, should he suddenly make his sister such a generous offer? 'I cannot help fancying he merely wants a *good servant* in Helen on his own terms.'

But Helen had made up her mind; and eventually, in floods of tears, set off for Dublin. She was succeeded by the ladylike Isabella, from Edinburgh, for whom Jane quickly found a nickname: Pessima—the worst. She was short-lived. Soon after the hysterics at the washtub she gave notice, protesting that if she were not allowed to leave the very next day she would take fits and be laid up in the house for a year. Jane, who was by this time laid up herself, made no attempt to stop her; and Isabella, smartly dressed and in high spirits, went off in an omnibus leaving her mistress in bed, with no one but the postman's wife, who came in temporarily, 'to oblige'.

Carlyle was soon complaining of discomfort. How much longer would it be before his shoes were cleaned and his library swept?

After an unfortunate experience with 'an old half dead cook' Jane put an advertisement in *The Times*, which produced a number of 'horrid looking females "inquiring after the place"—and one not horrid looking but a cheery little button of a creature' called Anne, whom she engaged. Anne had a follower, the butcher's boy; he 'came silently,' said Carlyle, 'and sat two hours once a week'. 'But they are a rational pair,' wrote Jane, 'and not likely to marry till he gets a business of his own.' 'Meanwhile,' she added, 'it rather pleases me to know of a little decent love-making going on in the house.' After the miseries she had been through with Helen, Anne's cheerful normality must have been a relief. She was a good cook, too, and had 'no tendency to drink'.

But Jane was soon complaining of her being 'a little slow, a little ineffectual'. She missed, she said, 'the enthusiasm, the *birr*, that was in Helen; the ready-to-fly-at-everything-ness; but on the other hand things go equably, without flare-ups. . . .'

At the end of two years the placid Anne married her faithful butcher and went off to Jersey. And at this juncture Jane received a letter from Helen. Her Irish adventure had ended in a violent quarrel with her brother, and she had gone back to Kirkcaldy where she had tried, unsuccessfully, to keep a small shop. She wanted to go back into service.

'We were glad to hear of Helen again,' said Carlyle, and Jane accepted what seemed a happy coincidence, and invited her to come back. Once again the cab drove up from St. Katherine's dock and deposited Helen and her belongings. This time her arrival must have seemed to her a homecoming. No doubt there were the old screams of joy and kissings of Jane from ear to ear; even the master came to greet her. 'The sight of Helen,' he said, 'was a glad sight of its kind.'

But it was not long before Jane knew that she had made a disastrous mistake. Helen's short-lived glory as mistress of her brother's house had done her immeasurable harm: she had grown careless and truculent. Moreover, Jane began to notice a slackening of control which at first she was at a loss to account for. The old

Helen whom she had befriended and encouraged—the endearing eccentric with her unpredictable commentary on persons and events—had undergone a depressing change. In Jane's eyes she had become degraded: she could only see her now as a servant—'a shocking dirty stupid servant', who could not, any more, be helped to improve. And Jane was not minded to help her: she suspected than Helen was beyond help. 'All morality is broken down in her', she wrote despairingly. 'I find now that she has not been even *honest* since she returned. . . .'

Within a few weeks the Carlyles learned only too clearly what was wrong. In February 1849 they went to spend a few nights with Captain Anthony Sterling at Headley Grove, near Betchworth, leaving Helen in charge of the house. Soon after midday on 19 February they returned in Captain Sterling's carriage, and knocked and rang at their own front door for some time without an answer.

'We were speculating about breaking a window and storming at Helen for having gone out when she knew we were coming,' wrote Jane, 'when the door opened to a twentieth blow and an apparition presented itself which I shall remember as long as I live. There stood Helen—her mouth all over blood, her brows and cheeks white with chalk from the kitchen floor—like an excessively ill got up stage ghost! her dark gown ditto—her hair hanging in two wild streams down her neck—her crushed cap all awry—and on her face a hideous smile of idiotic self-complacency! Nothing could be more drunk.'

Helen refused to go downstairs: she would not be 'used in that way', she declared; so Carlyle was obliged to drag her down to the kitchen, and leave her there on the floor. The house was filthy; the fires unlit. Helen had been drinking and giving parties all the time her employers had been away. 'The whole house was beastly,' said Jane. . . . 'That it escaped being either burnt or robbed is a miracle.'

Carlyle lit the parlour fire while Jane went in search of a temporary helper called Mrs. White, who seems to have taken control of the situation. She lit the kitchen fire 'and proceeded to get the dinner cooked' stepping round the recumbent Helen, who 'stormed at her for "daring to do *her* work" '.

Later in the day Helen managed to get on her feet, and 'rushed out into space,' said Jane, for more drink. This consisted of half a pint of rum and a quart of ale—in addition to the half-pint of gin she had taken in the morning. She came home in a state of collapse at ten o'clock, and Mrs. White, who seems to have been waiting up for her, 'got her into bed with difficulty,' and bolted her into the kitchen, before going home. But the bolt was not powerful enough to keep Helen indoors when the need for more drink seized her.

'When I came down at seven', wrote Jane, '. . . there was a sound as of an animal rolling on the kitchen stairs. The little beast had been out! with a bonnet and shawl on the top of her night clothes and had more drink.'

Jane refused to see her or speak to her; as soon as Helen was comparatively sober she was told by Mrs. White that she must get ready to leave the house next day.

This time there was no forgiveness to be wrung out of Jane. 'She tried her old despair and tears upon me—but in vain this time.' Finding her mistress unmoved, Helen took to her bed, swearing that no power on earth would induce her to leave Cheyne Row. At last, after Jane had threatened to send for a policeman and have her taken to the station, she agreed to dress herself and go to Camden Town 'to the house of her dearest friend' . . . who fortunately had a room to let. Jane took her there in Captain Sterling's carriage. It was a silent journey.

'I spoke hardly ten words to her all the way—explained the circumstances to the woman of the house—put two sovereigns into *her* hands, that she might pay herself the present shelter afforded her—and came away desiring never to see her (Helen) again in this world.'

'She may go to the Devil her own way,' added Jane. 'I have bothered myself enough in trying to hold her back.' But she went on bothering. 'Endless pains,' according to Carlyle, were taken and a new place found with a 'decent old widow in straitened circumstances, content to accept so much merit in a servant, and try to cure the drunkenness.'

'But nothing could save Helen!' he wrote. Away from Jane's influence, as she herself had predicted, she was lost. She made several attempts at suicide. 'She was once, as we heard, dragged from the river; did die, an outcast, a few months afterwards.'

So ended Helen's story. 'Poor bit dottle', wrote Carlyle by way of epitaph, 'what a history and tragedy in small!'

## CHAPTER FOUR

# In Sickness and in Health

WHEN their old servant Bessy Barnet made her dramatic re-appearance at Cheyne Row after nearly thirty years, she was shocked by Jane's haggard looks. She felt sure that there was something seriously wrong with her, and even, after their next meeting, went so far as to whisper the dread word 'cancer'. Jane pooh-poohed her fears—'Oh, Bessy! Bessy! just the same old woman!'—and accused her of morbid imaginings. But she agreed to go and spend a few days with the Blackistons at St. Leonards, where Bessy stuffed her with dainties—'calves foot jelly, etc., as if I were a young bird!' —and Doctor Blackiston gave her champagne and dosed her with pepsine to improve her appetite.

'Just the very latest caprice in medicine,' Jane called this. 'It is something scraped off the inside of people's stomachs (*dead* the

C.A.H.–D

people must be before one can conveniently scrape their stomachs!) or the stomachs of beasts for that matter (the *bear* stomach is understood to supply most of this something), and being scraped off, it is boiled and distilled, and bottled and sold and taken in drops; and the patient furnished with a fictitious gastric juice, which enables him to eat and digest like a bear! The Doctors here are prescribing it at no allowance; and the Druggists say they can't get enough for the demand.'

Dr. Blackiston's belief in the new drug was evidently no caprice, for a year later he was still urging Jane, 'Should your appetite fail, don't forget to take the pepsine.' But by this time she had found a new remedy: quinine. She had been taking it regularly, she said, twice a day, with good effect on her stomach. For anyone as easily depressed as Jane quinine seems a doubtful remedy; but it was mild in comparison with many of the drugs she took.

Her mother, as we have seen, dosed herself with pills; she also enjoyed dosing her daughter, and Jane, to put her in a good humour, swallowed a brew of senna pods when visiting Mrs. Welsh in 1836. 'One has fine times with my mother', she wrote, 'after an act of docility like that.'

For Carlyle, senna was mild; indeed, both Carlyles dosed themselves continually with castor oil and 'blue pills'; Carlyle resorted to castor oil whenever he was unwell, even taking it to allay his nervousness before lecturing.

'Carlyle should have had a "strong-minded woman" for a wife, with a perfectly sound liver, plenty of solid fat, and mirth and good humour without end', Jane wrote to her cousin Helen. 'I am too much like himself in some things—especially as to the state of our livers. . . .' And to her husband, 'To you as well as to me has a skin been given much too thin for the rough purposes of human life.'

They were both upset by journeys, by strange beds, by unwonted excitement. After one night away from home, in 1843, Carlyle returned 'with rheumatism in his back, nameless qualms in his interior—there has been the devil to pay ever since—and nothing less than a blue pill and a dose of castor oil have been needed, to counteract the quiet visit!'

In the early days of their marriage Carlyle thought of himself as a sick man: 'Perhaps one day', he wrote, 'I may triumph over long disease, and be myself again!' At this period he lost no opportunity of trying a new remedy; as we have seen, he submitted himself to a patent cure for indigestion invented by the chemist John Badams; and passing Lochinbreck Well in 1832, he 'drank a tumbler of arsenic water'. But the torments of indigestion went on, particularly when he was tired and overstrained, and, hopeless of permanent cure, he seems to have resisted further remedies (there is no record of pepsine being tried by him!), remaining constant to his castor oil and blue pill.

These blue pills contained mercury. In Chelsea they were regularly prescribed—half a grain for Mrs. Carlyle, five grains for her husband—and made up at intervals by Alsop the chemist. On one unfortunate occasion Carlyle was sent to order a fresh supply for Jane. The presence of another customer in the shop embarrassed him. Not liking to mention his wife's name in connexion with such things, 'The blue pills for our house,' he demanded loftily. 'So was *delicacy* another person's own reward', wrote Jane, while still weak from the overdose of mercury; for Alsop 'had preferred the masculine gender as grammatically bound to do' and made up Mr. Carlyle's prescription. That Jane recovered from the dose shows something for her powers of resistance. Carlyle attempted consolation with the thought that it might do her 'a great deal of good in the long run'; 'It may be strongly doubted,' Jane commented grimly, after being violently sick.

In the first days at Cheyne Row the health of both Carlyles improved. Jane was busy and happy. The novelty of life in London was stimulating to both. It was not till the winter that Jane's health began to decline; colds and headaches attacked her once more, and the following summer she had to be nursed back to health by her mother at Templand. In 1837 there was an influenza epidemic: Jane was a victim. Carlyle was determined not to have influenza: 'a dirty, feverish kind of cold,' he called it. 'I have set my face against it and said No.' This method was successful: he remained immune. In the same determined manner, a few years later, we find him confronting 'a little tickling in my nose which rapidly grew into a *sniftering*, and by the time next day came I had a regular ugly face-ache and fair foundation for cold in all its forms, which required to be energetically dealt with and resisted on the threshold'. After one day the cold had fled.

To all but his chronic afflictions, Carlyle was able to muster up a strong defence without the aid of medicines. He formulated his own ideas on health and hygiene and stuck to them through the years. In spite of the complaints in his early letters (we constantly hear of him being 'Dyspeptical, melancholic', 'sick with sleeplessness, nervous, bilious, splenetic'), he must have been constitutionally strong: it was his nerves that played the devil with him. And, like his wife, he could not help dramatizing his ailments. 'The mind is weary, the body is very sick; a little black speck dances to and fro in the left eye (part of the retina protesting against the liver, and striking work).' So he described himself after finishing the second volume of *The French Revolution*, adding that the little black speck must continue to flutter and dance in his eye till the book should be finished. It was always the same: while he was writing his nervous system was 'in a flame', and his health suffered; nevertheless, he never had a serious illness, and may be said to have proved the soundness of his theories as applied to his own health. His wife was less fortunate.

'He has a mania for fresh air, this man, and is never happy unless all the doors and windows are open.'

Jane complained bitterly of the draughts in which she was often obliged to sit, 'wearing a cloak and bonnet as if I were out of doors! . . . As he never takes cold himself,' she adds, 'he can't be made to understand how sitting between two open cross windows, at midnight, in an east wind, should not be excessively bracing and healthy for me.'

The back door, which opened eastwards into the garden, was another thorn in Jane's flesh. Carlyle liked it kept open, she declared, in all weathers: it made the whole house cold (she wrote one November), and brought on her cough when she had to go past it on her way to the kitchen. Even with doors and windows shut, the old house was draughty, especially when the east wind blew through it. Jane shivered and coughed, staying indoors in bad weather sometimes for weeks on end.

But cold winds did not trouble the Annandale philosopher in his layers of flannel and homespun. For him the open air was a necessity; he who in his youth had been out in all weathers on the Scottish moors often felt constricted inside the brick walls of Cheyne Row: even in the garden he was cramped, unable to breathe. Every summer it became necessary for him to escape, if possible to Scotland, where he could stride across open country or plunge into the sea.

Carlyle loved sea-bathing; he had been brought up to it and always benefited from it. He must have inherited this from his mother, of whom we hear at the age of 72, enjoying 'some sea-bathing about Arbigland'. Whenever possible he made for the sea, and Jane encouraged him, knowing that to be in or upon the sea did him more good than anything. But in the summer of 1841 his passion for the sea led to a disastrous holiday: Carlyle, his mother, Jane and Helen the maid spent a month in a cottage at Newby, on the Solway Firth—a wild lonely spot where their ears were filled unceasingly with 'the everlasting roar of the loud winds, and the coming and going of the great Atlantic brine'. The romantic poet in Carlyle who had cried aloud for a 'hut in the wilderness' was sadly disillusioned; the cottage was dirty, alive with fleas: Jane was miserable: the adventure cost him £70. 'We have quitted Newby', Jane wrote to John Forster, 'never to look upon its like again. . . . Oh, such a place! Never shall I forget its blood-red, moaning sea.'

But the longing to escape from London oppressed him continually. Prudence, he told his brother, bade him continue living in 'the pestiferous wen where my life is gaoled for these years'; nevertheless there were moods when he could endure London no longer. Jane felt that sometimes she was 'no longer in a *home* but in a *tent* to be struck any day that the commanding officer is sufficiently bilious'. She fought his moods of rebellion: for her Cheyne Row was precious and she clung to it. She had lived with Carlyle at Craigenputtock and knew that the peace he clamoured for would not be found in the wilderness. She encouraged him to ride and walk—to 'rush out into the solitary woods and green places' for the health of his body and the good of his soul. In 1839 a mare had been presented to him by an admirer: Carlyle was in two minds whether or no to keep her, the expense of feeding and stabling was considerable. Jane laughed at his fears. 'It is like buying a laying hen,' she said, 'and giving it to some deserving person. Accept it, dear!'

On Citoyenne, as he called her, he rode out over the old wooden Battersea Bridge and 'in ten minutes' swift trotting' was in the country lanes of Clapham and Wandsworth. From the wooded slopes of Sydenham he looked back over 'the monster', London, lying in the distance, 'quite buried, its smoke rising like a great dusky-coloured mountain, melting into the infinite clear sky. All is green, musical, bright. One feels that it is God's world this; and not an infinite Cockneydom of *stoor* and din after all.'

In August 1840 he set off, in cloak and broad-brimmed hat, with a knapsack on his back, a mackintosh strapped to the front of his saddle and a 'small round trunk the size of a quartern loaf' fastened on behind. He took a supply of pipes and tobacco and—though it was summer—dressed himself in clothes that the bad weather would not spoil. He was off for a week's riding tour in Sussex; and planned to make his way slowly to the coast, hoping to see 'the place where William the Conqueror fought and have one dip in the sea'.

'I shall be one of the most original figures!' he told his mother; and evidently this was so, for Jane entertained their friends years later with her account of his departure from Cheyne Row.

'She drew him,' said Froude disapprovingly, 'in her finest style of mockery—his cloak, his knapsack, his broad-brimmed hat, his preparation of pipes, etc.—comparing him to Dr. Syntax. He laughed as loudly as any of us: it was impossible not to laugh . . .' but Froude did not care for such displays of wit in a female. 'It struck me,' he said, 'as rather untender.'

After this successful tour Citoyenne was given up. 'The expense of a horse every day here is nearer four than three shillings,' Carlyle told his mother, 'far too heavy for a little fellow like me, whom even *it* does not make altogether healthy.' In future, he said, now and then he would 'get rolled out on a railway some twenty miles', and then walk for half a day.

But walking had not, for him, the charm of riding. Nor had the velocipede on which, with Gambardella, he rode to Wimbledon ('three hours,' said Jane, 'that strange pair were toiling along the Highways'). By 1845 he owned another horse—Black Duncan. 'I get considerable benefit of my horse, which is a very darling article, black, high, good-natured, very swift—and takes me out into the green country almost every day.'

Riding was worth the expense. It brought him escape from Cockneydom and it was beneficial to his liver. 'I don't believe Mr. C. could have lived through this Book',* Jane wrote years later, 'if it hadn't been for his horse exercise.'

She herself took 'carriage exercise' in broughams lent by friends —at the end of her life in her own brougham. And she was a great believer in long bus-rides, sometimes climbing on to the top of a horse omnibus and driving to Islington or Richmond. 'A good shilling's worth of exercise!' she called it. There is a charming picture of her in the spring of 1856, going off 'by two omnibuses to Hampstead, with Nero and a Book'. She spent several hours, she said, 'sitting on the Heath, and riding in a donkey-chair. The pleasantest thing I have tried for a long time.'

Towards the end of the 1850's a leaflet entitled *Hints Regarding Health and Disease* somehow made its way into the house. Carlyle read it through, leaving his written comments for all to see. The writer, he considered, was 'Better than some—though not very good', and he handed over the tract to the reigning servant-maid, Charlotte Southam. It is to be hoped that she observed the first hint—'Great cleanliness in the cooking of food'. 'To eat at regular hours—to eat moderately, and when the stomach is weak, to eat very little and frequently', were golden rules which Jane tried vainly to impose. But the final hints on preserving health—'To avoid all anxieties of the mind' and 'to cultivate a cheerful disposition' were unlikely to appeal to Carlyle.

Nor were the writer's views on smoking. He enumerated 'The

* *Frederick the Great.*

Disorders and Diseases produced by Tobacco', which were, he said, 'Loss of Appetite, Indigestion, Constipation, Headaches, Nervous Weakness.' ('Totally absurd', wrote Carlyle. 'Same may be said of oatmeal.') 'Irritability of temper', continued the tract, 'General Weakness of the faculties of Mind and Body, Despondency, Insanity, and Idleness of Mind and Body, that lead to innumerable evils.' What these were the author did not specify, but his opinion seems to have been that smoking was a mistake.

Carlyle disagreed. He smoked a great deal. At night when he could not sleep, or in the evening and early morning pacing up and down the garden. His pipes were laid in crevisses in the garden walls, and Anne Thackeray remembered, as a little girl, seeing them lying 'at intervals in the brickwork . . . all ready for use'.

When Jane first knew him, he smoked cigars; indeed, he stipulated that on the wedding journey from Templand to Edinburgh he should be allowed to smoke three, 'without criticism or reluctance, as things essential to my perfect contentment.' But it was pipe-smoking that became his chief solace, his soother of frayed nerves and aid to contemplation. According to his nephew Alexander, Carlyle never smoked while writing, and seldom while reading; tobacco was for him a means of relaxation, a much-needed narcotic.

'To keep the skin in a state of perfect purity by sponging daily with warm, tepid or cold water', was another recommendation of the tract-writer. Carlyle believed in cold water. His shower bath—a contraption of ropes and pulleys—was fixed into the ceiling of the back kitchen, where, standing in a tub, he hauled up bucketful after bucketful and emptied them over himself. Cold water was invigorating, strengthening, he believed; Jane was urged to try it, and we find her pouring a jug of cold water over the back of her neck to cure a headache. Then, in 1846, 'having found small profit hitherto in mending and tinkering at my *soul*, I am for the moment modestly directing my faculties to the repairing of my *body*. . . . Every morning I take the shower-bath—quite cold—and three pailfuls of it! The shock is indescribable! and whether it strengthens me or shatters me I have not yet made up my mind.'

For such fastidious people as the Carlyles, washing must have had its problems. The basin and jug in the bedroom were used for daily ablutions, with probably an added jug of hot water carried up from the kitchen. There was a hip-bath, in which ablutions of a more ambitious sort were carried out, with the aid of several jugfuls of hot water: there is no record of this ritual, but it almost certainly took place at least once a week, in both bedrooms, after which the hip-bath would be laboriously emptied, and removed.

Sanitation was primitive: 'slops' would be poured down the drain in the yard; the bedrooms were furnished with chamber-pots, and there was an earth closet in the garden. In these ways the house had hardly changed during a hundred and fifty years: the only improvement was the introduction of main water in 1852, when a tap in the basement kitchen superseded the pump. But the problems of washing and sanitation remained the same, and personal cleanliness was a matter of great discomfort and hard work for both master and servant.

'Jane Carlyle has eight influenzas annually,' said Harriet Martineau; and though Jane indignantly denied the accusation, there was some truth in it. The London winters and the damp foggy atmosphere of Chelsea affected her; by 1848 she was resorting to opium to cure a persistent cough. At the same time she was taking morphia for sleeplessness. Victorian remedies often sound drastic; but there is no doubt that Jane dosed herself with a recklessness that defeated its own end. The morphia she took increased the state of nervous tension in which she was living, and aggravated the fears —fears of losing her husband's affection, fears of mortal disease, fears of becoming insane—with which she gradually became obsessed.

In the early days of her marriage Jane's belief in Carlyle's genius and the pleasure she took in organizing her frugal household gave her purpose and fulfilment. Since her girlhood she had suffered at intervals from agonizing headaches, but her slow decline in health began after Carlyle had become a celebrity, when—no longer able to work for his success, or even to share his ambitions, and often feeling herself thrust aside—she was cast more and more upon her own resources, and unconsciously took refuge in hypochondria.

She was no *malade imaginaire*. Indeed, her will was often stronger than her ailments. In 1843 she rose from her sick-bed to go to a party at the Macreadys'. ('My dear,' Carlyle said, 'I think I never saw you look more bilious; your face is *green* and your eyes all bloodshot.') After a riotous evening, with Thackeray, Dickens and Forster all at the top of their form, she returned in the small hours and 'slept like a top!!! plainly proving that excitement is my rest'.

Twenty years later, after a street accident had shocked and lamed her, she became seriously ill. Carlyle was immersed in *Frederick the Great* and she was removed from Cheyne Row to St. Leonards in a vehicle which looked like a hearse; she felt that she would never return. The sea air was of no avail; her condition grew steadily worse and Dr. Blackiston was unable to help her. With an immense effort, for at times her only wish was to die, she made up her mind that if she were to go on living, she must get to Scotland. John Carlyle, her doctor brother-in-law, offered to accompany her. Buoyed up by champagne and the power of her will, she survived the long exhausting train journey, which cannot have been eased by her companion.

'John was dreadfully ill-tempered: we quarrelled incessantly', she wrote. But perhaps her tactless brother-in-law acted as a counter-irritant, for 'my horrible ailment,' she added, 'kept off as if by enchantment'. The pain and the longing to put an end to herself which had tortured her night after night at St. Leonards, were kept at bay. At Carlisle she 'took a good breakfast', and John had the grace to apologize for his bad temper.

But a week later he upset her again. The pain had returned; but Doctor Carlyle took an unsympathetic view of Jane's ill health.

'Fancy him telling me in my agony yesterday that if I had ever done anything in my life this would not have been; that no poor woman with work to mind had ever such an ailment as this of mine since the world began!'

Perhaps there was an element of truth in this blunt statement; though it was hardly the thing to say to a woman fighting for her life. Jane had suffered, for years, from the frustration of an artist who cannot find his *métier*. The household tasks, the feverish rearranging and redecorating of the house, the fussing over 'Mr. C's' meals, were not enough to occupy her quick mind: she was often bored. She knew—and Carlyle never ceased to reiterate the same philosophy—that idleness begot misery, that her salvation, mental and spiritual, lay in work. But what work? 'I tell her many times,' said Carlyle, 'there is much for her to do if she were trained for it: her whole sex to deliver from the bondage of frivolity, dollhood and imbecility, into the freedom of valour and womanhood.' Fine words! But what could the dutiful Victorian wife be trained to do? And Jane was dutiful. It was her duty to entertain the bores that Carlyle would not see; it was equally her duty to mend his clothes and see to his meals. She submitted, and her frustrated brilliance was poured into letter-writing, as were her stored-up miseries and some of her unspoken fears.

In her letters Jane dramatized many of her afflictions—but there is no doubt of the reality of her sufferings. She was acutely sensitive, neurotic: pain, when it came, was violent and overwhelmed her. In the throes of one of her headaches she clutched Carlyle so wildly that a ring fell from her finger into his dressing-gown pocket. In October 1856 a 'fearful pain' in her left side was so intense that she could not stop screaming. 'Who shall I send for? what shall I do?' Carlyle asked. But she could only gasp between screams, 'Nobody, nobody, only put me into hot water.' She had been taking morphia. 'And I can assure Dr. Russell', she wrote to his wife, 'I *am* "very ill" when I scream—not to say scream without intermission for half an hour together!!'

Throughout the 1850's the words 'morphia' and 'morphine' occur at regular intervals in her letters. It is easy to understand why: morphia did bring relief of a kind, and usually induced oblivion—'as near an approach to the blessed state of *Nirvana* as anyone not a worshipper of Buddha need aspire to'. In 1851 she accidently took an overdose. The morphine was made up into pills; taking some out after an interval she found that 'the little black pills had melted and run all together and I had to divide them with a penknife. All next day I felt quite *dead* . . . and at night I took to fainting and having horrid spasms.'

All this time she had not sent for a doctor. Their first Chelsea doctor, who had advised that Jane 'should be kept always happy and tranquil', was dead, and she had not tried another. In September 1856 she went to stay with old friends, Dr. and Mrs. Russell at Thornhill; they were concerned to find her taking morphia. The doctor tried to break her of it and recommended a tablespoon of whisky in hot milk; and while she was in Scotland and in the soothing company of Mary Russell, this did give her some sleep. But back in London she caught a chill, which developed itself into a violent cold 'with tetanic complications', and after four sleepless nights resorted again to morphia. She apologized to Mary Russell for 'being so cowardly'. 'Don't let him (the Doctor) fancy I make a practice of taking morphia whenever I can't sleep; I hadn't taken any for months.'

'I hardly ever begin to write here', she noted in the short journal she kept in 1855, 'that I am not tempted to break out into Jobisms about my bad nights. . . . Oh, to cure anyone of a terror of annihilation, just put him on my allowance, and see if he don't get to long for sleep, sleep, unfathomable and everlasting sleep as the only conceivable heaven.'

She tried henbane. She swallowed chloroform. But she could not give up morphia, even though its after-effects were often unpleasant. 'Two morphia pills', in 1853, brought on sickness, followed by 'retching and fainting'. She had to spend a day in bed, and even then was 'too weak for anything'. After Dr. Russell's warnings she tried whisky, wine, gin: once, in Scotland, 'a *stiff* little tumbler of Hollands Toddy' gave her 'the soundest longest sleep' she had had for years. But always, *in extremis,* she took morphia. Carlyle was sympathetic but uneasy. 'Glad I am', he wrote, 'that the subtle Morphine has done its function; be thankful to it, tho' *beware* also!' But when a bout of sleeplessness overtook her she could heed no warnings: she was desperate, reckless. Once thirty drops—'an exceptional dose' as she called it—had no effect. But the following night the drug did its work, giving her 'a sleep so deep and so long, that when I awoke from it I hadn't an atom of recollection *who* I was! Was clear about nothing but only that it couldn't be *me* who had that nice sleep!!'

In April 1859 she was driven at last to call in a doctor; she had
had her usual influenza and was unable to throw it off. 'Sleepless,
foodless, coughing, tormented somewhere in the region of the heart,
she has been as ill as I ever saw her', Carlyle wrote to his brother
John. The nearest general practitioner was Dr. Barnes in the King's
Road. Fortunately, Jane took a fancy to him. 'He finds me,' she said,
'the very oddest patient he ever had.' To Carlyle he said that of all
the patients he had ever had Jane was the most excitable. Tonics,
wine, and nourishing food were what Dr. Barnes considered she
needed. She was to have complete rest: 'not to write, or read, or
talk, or think! above all, I was "on no account to *think*!" I might knit
in my bed, but nothing else.' Unfortunately Jane had never learnt
to knit.

The following New Year Dr. Barnes sent in his bill. Carlyle, in
paying it, wrote:

'Dear Sir,

Enclosed is a draught for your account,—which I have very much
pleasure in paying, with a great many thanks over and above. No
man of the many who present themselves at this season has done so
essential a service during the past year; and none of them all could
do his poor "work" more like a workman than you did your high
and important one! We wish you many good years useful to your
fellow creatures and yourself.

  'I am always
    'Yours sincerely,
     Thomas Carlyle.'

That year, 1860, the long strain of Carlyle's labours on *Frederick
the Great*—the 'valley of the shadow of Frederick', Jane called it—
began to take its toll on both husband and wife. Since its conception
in 1851 the whole household had been in a constant state of tension
supporting the immense physical and mental effort endured by the
master, who struggled on upstairs in the prolonged birth-pangs of
this last monster child whom he grew to hate. 'Frederick' was not
finished till 1865, after thirteen years of work.

In August 1860 Carlyle went to Scotland. 'I trust in God he will
get calmed down by a good long stay there', wrote Jane. She

remained in Chelsea, uncertain what to do. 'His nervous state had acted upon me, till I was become more sleepless and agitated than himself! And I was on the verge of complete breakdown into serious illness when Mr. C. left, and my Doctor took me into his hands.' Dr. Barnes prescribed 'composing draughts' three times a day, and begged her not to go away till she was stronger. 'Beware of over-working that excited brain of yours,' he said, and wrote out a prescription for a medicine which looked like blue paint, and which worked like magic on a sore throat. For physical ills Dr. Barnes was always ready with a remedy. He did not prescribe many medicines, but was a great believer in a very nourishing diet—plenty of meat: 'Juicy mutton chops and that sort of thing,' said Jane; 'and two glasses a day of good sherry.' She was also encouraged to drink 'new milk' with a tablespoonful of rum in it. During a bout of sickness and nausea (after the pepsine treatment at St. Leonards) Jane took to her bed, unable to eat a thing. Dr. Barnes was sent for ('Mr. C. never being alarmed at any form of illness but the incapacity of taking one's regular meals', wrote Jane). The kindly doctor said she was upset by the hot weather, and put mustard blisters on her stomach, ordering a diet of soda water with a little brandy. After a week she was about again, as she said 'after a sort', but feeling weak as a dishclout.

But in the long illness that overtook her in 1863, Dr. Barnes confessed himself defeated. He had been treating her for the injury she received after her unlucky fall in St. Martin's-le-Grand when 'a furious cab', as Carlyle put it, had caused her to lose her balance, and fall in the street wrenching the sinews of her left thigh. The pain was acute, far worse, said Dr. Barnes, than if she had broken the bone. The agony was beyond the reach of 'composing draughts'; but after a week it grew more endurable and Dr. Barnes made her get out of bed 'for fear of a bad back'. Soon she was walking, 'using one of the maids as a crutch', and the Doctor began to talk of getting her away for a change of air. He was unprepared for the reaction to this accident of his patient's overstrained nervous system. Before it happened she had already been suffering a great deal of pain in her left arm, which had been diagnosed by Lord Ashburton's physician

Dr. Quain as 'neuralgia'. She had been driven to consult him while staying with the Ashburtons, and he had prescribed quinine pills, and sent her an embrocation of opium, aconite, camphor and chloroform. Dr. Barnes ignored the pain in her arm, said she had influenza.

'It seems to me he regards my leg as his patient, and my arm as Dr. Quain's patient, which he has nothing to do with', Jane wrote to Mrs. Russell. But he recommended bark and soda—'one of the most nauseous mixtures he knew of in this world'—as being better than the quinine Dr. Quain prescribed—'your ladylike quinine', he called it.

But nothing, bark, quinine, embrocation or 'nourishing diet' could hold back the 'deluge of intolerable pain, indescribable unaidable pain', as Carlyle put it, which gradually overwhelmed her. No doctor could ease her: no doctor really knew what was wrong. 'Neuralgia' was Dr. Quain's name for her illness: Dr. Barnes called it rheumatism. Dr. Blackiston at St. Leonards sent her a prescription for iodide of potash, to be taken with quantities of fluid, together with pills of valeriate or quinine. She could not lift her arm, and was in constant pain, suffering too from not knowing the cause of her malady, imagining it to be angina pectoris, paralysis, disease of the spine. . . .

She was sent to St. Leonards where Dr. Blackiston prescribed a new liniment and 'rubbing with opium'. But she had no faith in any treatment now. 'Dr. B.', she wrote, 'knows nothing more about it than the other doctors.'

She had little hope of recovery. 'Oh my Dear, my Dear!' she wrote to her husband, 'shall I ever make fun for you again? Or is our life together indeed past and gone? I want so much to *live*—to be to you more than I have ever been; but I fear, I fear!'

Carlyle packed his books into a vast wooden crate and removed himself and *Frederick* to St. Leonards. Dr. Barnes—'poor bewildered Mr. Barnes'—visited her there. He could do nothing. This was an illness of the nerves. The disease, he said, would burn itself out. Dr. Blackiston gave her a new sort of 'blue pill' to help her to sleep. She went for long drives. But she grew steadily worse, more sleepless, more desperate.

It was not until she had made up her mind to move from St. Leonards and travel to Scotland that the note of panic in her letters begins to diminish. She had been in terror of going insane; she had begged Dr. Quain to give her the means to do away with herself.

On 22 July 1864, she parted from John Carlyle and his unhelpful advice, and her friend Mary Russell carried her off to Thornhill. Here, in the soothing atmosphere of the Russells' house, and under the care of these good friends, her shattered nerves were eased. She began to sleep again, for an hour or two; she began to put on a little weight. 'When weighed last Friday I was found to have gained a pound and a half in ten days!!!' But she was very weak, and could hardly walk a step. Dr. Russell made her 'exercise her legs': 'I do my best,' she wrote; 'but no good seems to come of it.' Then, on 19 August she wrote to her husband: 'Something occurred here last evening between the hours of eight and nine, which produced an extraordinary sensation! Mrs. Russell has not got over it yet! My Dear, I *laughed*!!!!'

'I think ye're gaun to get better noo!' said the little housemaid one morning when she brought up Jane's glass of milk. At Holm Hill everything was sunny, calm, optimistic. The bad nights still persisted, but what she called 'the special misery'—the terror of insanity and thoughts of self-destruction—grew less, would certainly 'wear itself out in time' Dr. Russell told her. She read a chapter on 'Neuralgia' in one of his medical books in which a case was quoted of a patient 'bent on self destruction'. 'It was a sort of comfort to me', wrote Jane, 'to find that my dreadful wretchedness was a not uncommon feature of my disease, and not merely an expression of individual cowardice.'

On 1 October she came home. The train was late, and when the cab drove down Cheyne Row, Carlyle, desperately anxious, rushed out into the street in his dressing-gown, 'and kissed me, and wept over me . . . (much to the edification of the neighbours at their windows, I have no doubt)'. The two maids appeared behind him, 'with flushed faces and tears in their eyes'.

There was no doubt now that she was better. 'They were all

astonished,' she said, 'at the improvement in my appearance.' That first night at home after so many months she slept like a top— 'sleep,' she called it, 'for only the angels, and for the mortal who had travelled from three to four hundred miles through the night!' She was soon putting the house to rights, straightening the pictures which were 'hung up all crooked' and mourning over the broken china and pots and pans. Within a fortnight she had sacked the housemaid.

Her friends showered her with kindness. The Rector's wife, Mrs. Blunt, offered a daily tumbler of fresh milk from a cow she kept for her children. 'She has kindly included me,' said Jane, 'as "the biggest and best child"; and with a key into their garden my cook can run to their stable with a tumbler and be back at my bedside in ten minutes.' The house was filled with flowers. 'It is impossible to tell who is kindest to me,' she told her sister-in-law; 'my fear is always that I shall be stifled with roses.' 'I cannot tell you', she wrote at the end of this letter, 'how gentle and good Mr. Carlyle is! He is as busy as ever, but he studies my comfort and peace as he never did before.'

The end of the dark Valley of the Shadow of Frederick was near: Jane had never expected to see it.

## CHAPTER FIVE

# Neighbours and Nuisances

NUMBER 6, the house next door on the north side, was a house full of mysteries. Jane amused Dickens with stories of the goings-on there; 'I have thoughts of writing a novel about it,' she said in 1865. During the thirty years she had known it, number 6 had been inhabited by a series of tenants who provided over the years a series of shocks.

In the spring of 1839 a family called Lambert moved in, bringing with them, Jane noted in horror, 'an accumulation of all the things to be guarded against in a London neighbourhood, viz., a pianoforte, a lap-dog, and a parrot'. The two first, she said, could be borne with, as they 'carry on their glory within doors'; but the parrot was put out in the garden, where it held forth, screeching and making all the noises parrots make under the open windows of number 5. At last Carlyle 'fairly sprang to his feet, declaring he could "neither think nor live" '. 'Now it was absolutely necessary,' continued Jane, 'that he should do both. So forthwith, on the inspiration of conjugal sympathy I wrote a note to the parrot's mistress (name unknown), and, in five minutes after, Pretty Polly was carried within, and is now screeching from some subterranean depth whence she is hardly audible.' This was an easy victory: but the parrot was only the beginning of the troubles from number 6.

This house belonged to two brothers named Martin, one of whom, Carlyle said, 'had fallen imbecile'; since when number 6 was let, and continued to be let, to a succession of increasingly down-at-heel tenants. When the Lamberts moved away the house had begun to fall into disrepair, and was evidently allowed to remain neglected. For some years it was overrun by a cheerful feckless Irish family called Ronca, with 'mechanic sons-in-law' who hammered and sawed in the back garden while female members of the tribe dragged out large wash-tubs and strung lines of laundry from wall to wall. But worse was to follow. When the sons-in-law had knocked together some coops, an assortment of poultry was introduced, including, to Jane's dismay, several cocks.

Carlyle had, by this time, become fanatical about noise. Even when they were first married and living at Comely Bank, Edinburgh, Jane had been obliged to write polite notes requesting the silencing of 'an old maid's house-dog and an only son's pet bantam cock'. Now, some twenty years later, Carlyle could not write, could not think, could not sleep or concentrate on anything except giving vent to his rage, if he heard certain sounds. He was selective: cocks and pianos were his chief enemies. A cock crowing in the small hours woke him instantly: he would thump his bed in his wrath, then jump up and pace the room, waiting furiously for the next crow, which would sometimes drive him out of the house, to walk about the streets till morning.

Jane was also a light sleeper: staying in Suffolk, in August 1842, she wrote: 'Every night brings forth some new variety of assassin to murder sleep!' One night it was the church bell, another 'an ass, or several asses, braying as if the devil were in them'. Soon she was complaining of 'braying, lowing, crowing, cackling, barking, howling'. Compared with this quiet country parsonage, Cheyne Row was silent as the grave; but the cocks that woke Carlyle invariably woke Jane, for she slept immediately below him, and would lie awake listening to the angry thumpings and stumpings, waiting for the final stampede downstairs and the slam of the hall door. As she waited her mind was active with plans for the 'extinguishing' of the bird next day. This meant calling upon the owner, explaining her husband's nervous condition and trying to arrange for the cock to be shut up indoors during the night: 'efforts that I still shudder at the recollection of', she wrote afterwards.

Several cocks in neighbouring gardens had been silenced in this way. But in the case of the Roncas' 'Demon Fowls' neither bribes nor entreaties brought about any lasting improvement. The Roncas could not, or would not, co-operate. Things grew worse when a macaw named Sara joined the menagerie. The cocks continued to crow by night, Sara shrieked by day, and the Roncas blandly disregarded Mrs. Carlyle's appeals. Finally Carlyle, raging against 'the infernal cocks', fled with Jane to the Ashburtons' house in Hampshire.

But the problem could not be allowed to drop. Jane, exhausted with worry, suggested desperately that they should try and take over number 6 themselves: 'turn Ronca with his vermin out of it, and let it stand empty—empty and noiseless. What is £40 or £45 a year, to saving one's life and sanity?' Rather to her dismay, Carlyle took up her suggestion with enthusiasm: she had better go straight back to London and arrange things. Jane's heart sank. 'I thought it a most wild-goose enterprise I was sent on, and when Lady Ashburton . . . asked him why he sent poor me instead of going himself, . . . he coolly answered, "Oh, I should only spoil the thing, she is sure to manage it".'

She did manage it. 'Before the week was out I had done better than take a house we did not need, for I had got the people bound down legally "under a penalty of ten pounds, and of immediate notice to quit, never to keep, or allow to be kept, fowls, or macaw, or other nuisance on the premises", in consideration of five pounds given them by Mr. Carlyle.' She had used all her charm on the house agent, Mr. Owlton, to achieve this victory; and when the agreement was put into her hand she burst into tears, and would have kissed the man, she said, if he had not been so ugly.

And now for more than ten years the neighbouring gardens were 'quite cleared' of cocks. But in 1865 history, at number 6, repeated itself. By this time a new tenant had moved in—'a very mysterious "dressmaker" ,' who took in very mysterious lodgers. The last to come was a lady who arrived with two vanloads of furniture, 'which being all carried in, the shutters of the lower room were closed and have never been opened since!!' Jane's curiosity was aroused—and also her apprehensions. Her dressing-room commanded a view of all that went on in number 6's garden, which by this time had degenerated into a sordid patch of weeds and rubbish. Here, she said 'phenomena' now presented themselves—'from which we could infer—several things!! For example, an exceptionally bad old rocking horse with a tattered side saddle, indicated the neighbourhood of a female child, who, added to the solitary little boy of the dressmaker, very quiet boy hitherto, might get up more noise than Mr. C. would like. Then, an enormous trap-wired cage, taken out to be cleaned, left no doubt of—*a parrot*, good God! There was a prospect for us when the fine weather came and this accursed bird should be hung outside to produce the horriblest sounds.'

It was Sara and the Roncas all over again. But the parrot was not all. 'A number of green spars of unequal lengths, mixed up with mats and wicker boxes', were translated overnight into a henhouse. When Jane looked out next morning, there, 'airing themselves in the garden', were nine hens—and one magnificent cock, 'who, bewildered by the novelty of his position maintained a golden silence. But I knew,' she added grimly, 'whether that was likely to last.'

She was right. The next night, in the small hours, 'a loud crow seemed to issue from under my bed' and was repeated three times. The same performance, she said, was repeated hourly, 'Mr. C. sleeping soundly through it all, and with my heart thumping, listening, not for the crowing only, but far worse, for Mr. C's. step on the floor overhead, telling me he had been disturbed and would make everybody know he had. Oh my heavens!' Night after night the cock crowed and Jane lay sleepless: for a whole week, she said, she bore her hideous secret in her heart. Mr. C. made no sign, having by this time forgotten about cocks, and being free, as Jane put it, to devote his exclusive attention to railway whistles. It was only when, happening to glance out of his dressing-room window, he saw the cock, that his rage broke forth.

But Jane had taken action. She had, as of old, 'eaten dirt', and negotiations had been entered into with number 6. Once again, Jane's diplomacy triumphed: the dressmaker agreed to have the poultry removed within a week; and meanwhile the cock would be shut up in the coal cellar every night. Not a crow would issue from him till after the Carlyles had breakfasted. 'And all I have to pay for this restoration of peace and quietness is giving a lesson, three times a week, in syllables of two letters, to a small Irish boy'—the dressmaker's son, who, said his mamma, was 'too excitable' to be sent to school. 'Meanwhile,' wrote Jane, 'Mr. C. declares me to be his "guardian angel". No sinecure, I can tell him.'

It was no sinecure; but by this time she was used to the job. For more than thirty years she had waged a perpetual war against noise.

The piano that arrived with the Lambert family in 1839 did not begin to give serious trouble for a year or two. Perhaps at first, like Jane's, it was kept on the ground floor where the front parlour of number 6 was divided from that of number 5 by the width of the hall. In this position it would, as Jane said, 'carry on its glory' quietly enough. But by 1842 the piano-playing had become a menace, and there was no doubt at all where the piano was. It was upstairs in the front drawing-room, with only a panelled wall between it and Carlyle, at work in his study.

Miss Lambert could be heard having a music lesson once a week, and on other days practising in a desultory way, sitting down for a few minutes at a time and running over a piece, or part of a piece. She seemed to have a good deal of free time, particularly in the mornings, when Carlyle was at work. In the early mornings she played scales, and soon, like the four-and-twenty blackbirds when the pie was opened, she began to sing.

One morning, 'in a *fix*' as Jane put it, with his writing, and unable to endure the spasmodic tinkling any longer, Carlyle 'took up the poker, and with the head of it gave two startling blows on the wall "exactly opposite where he fancied the young Lady seated". The music—if music it can be called—ceased in a moment, and all was quiet as death in No. 6 for the next twelve hours!'

But Miss Lambert was too enthusiastic a musician to be quelled for long. 'Oh that horrible squalling girl!' wrote Jane two weeks later. 'In these wet days she is worse than ever! Every morning that I get leave to sleep a little longer than usual she rattles me up with her accursed scales vocal and instrumental!' It was not the early scales, however, but the desultory tinkling that issued at un-predictable intervals through the study wall which finally resolved Carlyle to take action. He made up his mind to write the young lady a letter. Jane did not see this missive before it went, and clearly had misgivings; 'but he gave me to understand that it was of the most chivalrous description professing his conviction that "a young beautiful female soul working in the most beautiful element that of *music* would not willingly give annoyance to any fellow worker!!" etc. etc.' Miss Lambert was asked to refrain from playing till after two o'clock—'a modest request,' commented Jane, 'to a young lady whose whole existence seems to be in practising'.

The answer to this appeal was a visit from the musician's papa. When Helen announced him Jane feared that he had come 'to make a shine'. But the first glance at him as he entered reassured her. 'We have had a delightful day, Mam!' observed Mr. Lambert politely as he sat down. But Jane was not going to waste time talking about the weather. 'I led the conversation to the piano—saying that my husband had been invading his house today with a most unheard-of remonstrance—but the amiable gentleman would not let me finish— he bewailed the annoyance his daugh*ters* must have given us. . . .' So there were two piano-playing Miss Lamberts! No wonder the pianoforte had been thumped so energetically and so often. But the father was prepared to 'do unheard of things' to improve the situation. The instrument would be moved away from the wall—the top should be kept shut—there should be 'no playing in the forenoons' . . . 'When Carlyle came,' continued Jane, 'Mr. Lambert seemed ready to fall on his knees before him to implore his forgiveness for having daughters who played on the piano.' The visit ended in a flourish of handshaking and civil speeches, and next day the piano— played 'as if for trial for about a minute'—was barely audible. 'Heaven knows,' said Jane, 'how they have deadened the sound.'

The successful 'putting down' of the Lambert piano so encouraged Carlyle that for the first time he announced his intention of settling down at Cheyne Row. By May 1843, to Jane's astonishment, he was talking of buying the house, in order, he said, to be able to build a workroom at the end of the garden, or a 'well deafened observatory' at the top of the house. He had grand plans for throwing the study and Jane's bedroom into one large drawing-room. 'He would like,' wrote Jane incredulously, 'he would like, he says, to have a soirée now and then!! "once a fortnight or so"!! Is he going mad? or is it I who have been mad all this while in fancying that he disliked company—and cared nothing about "appearances"? . . . I am at my wits' end! My bedroom turned into a drawing room—soirées once a fortnight with *one maid* servant? the realisation of these wild dreams is still a great way off—but I confess they appal me!'

The house was not bought: Mr. Morgan of Pope's Head Alley could not be persuaded to part with the lease. Nevertheless, that summer Jane seized the opportunity of Carlyle's being invited to stay in Wales, to subject the house to what she called an earthquake. It was a good chance to make some improvements, less ambitious than Carlyle's, but more in keeping with her own ideas of what was needed and what could be afforded.

In the study more bookcases must be put in, and a better grate; and as the room was to be used for entertaining she must refurnish it more elegantly. Since her mother's death the year before, furniture had come from Templand. Mrs. Welsh's Chippendale chairs could now take the place of the cheap cane ones, which would do for the bedrooms. Also for the new study-drawing-room there were 'a sofa, easy chair, ottoman, cushions, stools—every conceivable luxury!' all of which Jane planned to cover herself in chintz while the earthquake was in progress. There was a great deal to be done: the house needed a thorough cleaning, carpets taken up and beaten and curtains taken down and washed; Carlyle would have to be away at least a month.

Pearson, the builder in Church Street, was called in, and given his orders. Jane decided to do away with the 'queer old press' on the left of the study chimney-breast. This was in fact a closet, about 5 feet by 4 feet with a long narrow window overlooking the street; its removal would make the room larger and lighter. The ceiling was to be whitewashed, the room door 'turned' so that it opened from left to right—and the upper part of the Queen Anne panelling filled in with canvas and papered. Jane chose a wall-paper with a pink and white design and arranged for the wainscot and skirting to be painted and varnished. The panelled walls of the staircase and hall were also to be repainted, and all the ceilings whitewashed.

On 3 July Carlyle went off to Clifton on his way to Wales. 'He has no idea how long he will stay or whether he will come straight back or go round by Scotland—or the moon!' Jane wrote to her cousin Jeannie. And to her husband she was soon writing, 'Well, you cannot come back here at all rates,—that is flat.'

Alone at Cheyne Row, with only Helen for protection, she armed herself at night with a dagger and a policeman's rattle. There had been robberies in the district, and she noticed for the first time how easy it would be for an agile thief to climb into her bedroom: but she refused to be alarmed. 'The first night is over', she wrote, having woken at four and taken a blue pill, 'and we are neither robbed nor murdered.' Anyway, there was no time to speculate about thieves; Pearson's men were to start work next day: with Helen's help she must 'prepare the criminal for execution'.

On 5 July, at six in the morning, a 'legion of devils' rushed in and took possession of the house—'a painter, two carpenters, a paper-hanger, two nondescript apprentice-lads, and a "spy" '. Soon the house was uninhabitable. The smell of paint was appalling. Fortunately the weather was warm, so at night she slept, in open defiance of robbery, with all her windows wide; rose early and took a shower bath, and spent the day out of doors. She built herself a 'sort of Gipsy's tent' in the garden, with washing poles, clothes lines and an old brown floor cloth, 'under which remarkable shade I sit in an armchair at a small round table, with a hearth-rug for carpet under my feet, writing materials, sewing-materials, and a mind superior to Fate!' Every now and then the tent fell down on top of her, but she bore with this inconvenience, happy to escape from 'the abominable paint-smell, and the infernal noise within doors'.

The noise was indescribable. As well as the inevitable sawings and hammerings, and the whistling and singing of the men as they clattered up and down the uncarpeted stairs, all the old paint had to be rubbed off with pumice stone, which made a noise 'as it were a hundred knife-grinders melted into one': this job was given to the apprentices. One of these lads, scraping away at the paint in the hall, consoled himself under the hideous task, said Jane, 'by striking up every two minutes "The Red Cross Knight" or "Evelyn's Bower" or some such plaintive melody, which, after a brief attempt to render itself predominant, dies away into an unintelligible whinner'.

'It is only *I*', Jane wrote to Carlyle, 'who can be "jolly" in such a mess of noise, dirt and wild dismay! I said to the lad in the lobby, this morning, who was filling the whole house with "Love's Young Dream", "how *happy* you must feel that can sing thro' that horrible noise you are making!" "Yes, thank you, Ma'am," says he, "I'm happy enough *so far as I knows,* but I's always a-singing anyhow! it sounds pleasant to sing at one's work, doesn't it, Ma'am?" "Oh, very pleasant," said I, quite conquered by his simplicity: "but it would be still pleasanter for *me* at least, if you would sing a song from beginning to end, instead of bits here and there." "Thank you, Ma'am," says he again; "I'll try." ' 'But', she added, 'he does not succeed.'

Carlyle was persuaded to remain away. 'The stairs are all flowing with whitewash', wrote Jane, 'and altogether, when I fancy you here "in the midst of it", I do not know whether to laugh, or to cry, or to shriek.'

'But it will be a clean pretty house for you to come home to,' she continues; 'and should you find that I have exceeded by a few pounds your modest allowance for painting and papering, you will find I have not been thoughtless nevertheless, when I show you a document from Mr. Morgan, promising to "indemnify us for the same in the undisturbed possession of our house for five years!" '

This was a smart piece of business on Jane's part, and she was proud of herself. 'Old Sterling' (chief leader-writer of *The Times*), drove her to Pope's Head Alley and was present at the interview with Mr. Morgan, who, as well as owning the house, was a lawyer. She came away with a piece of paper equivalent to a lease of the house for five years 'with the reciprosity all on one side, binding him and leaving us free. "Such a thing," old Sterling said . . . "as no woman but myself would have had the impudence to ask, nor any lawyer in his senses the folly to grant." ' Jane was convinced that 'no such beatific vision as that of a real live woman, in a silk bonnet and muslin gown, ever irradiated that dingy, dusty law-chamber of his, and sat there on a three-feet-high stool, since he had held a pen behind his ear; and certainly never before had either man or woman, in that place, addressed him as a human being, not as a lawyer, or he would not have looked at me so struck dumb with admiration when I did so'.

This Dickensian character had never heard of Carlyle. 'He asked me,' said Jane, 'if your name were John or William—plainly he had lodged an angel unawares.'

By 3 August, Carlyle's library was finished. While the earthquake rumbled on downstairs, Jane sat in the clean, newly-furnished room and wrote to her husband. 'I feel like a little Queen', she told him; 'indeed, I suppose no Queen ever got half the comfort out of a nice room; Queens being born to them as the sparks fly upwards.' 'There are still some finishing strokes to be given,' she adds, 'the bookshelves all to be put up, and the window curtains; and a deal of needlework has to go to the last. But when all is done, it will be such a pleasure to receive you and give you tea in your new library!'

Five days later, feeling that she had earned a rest, she accepted an invitation to join Old Sterling in the Isle of Wight. Unhappily this little holiday, which might have been so agreeable, was ruined for Jane by the old man's determination upon a cheap lodging. After one night at Ryde in what he called 'the dearest hotel in Europe', his valet was sent out to look for lodgings and eventually, after much weighing of prices, the old man engaged 'a small but neat sitting-room, with two bedrooms', 'of which,' said Jane, 'the roomiest was assigned to me—plainly in the expectation that I should modestly prefer the inferior one. But not at all,' she went on; 'my modesty remained perfectly passive. . . . If he chose to make a sacrifice of comfort for so paltry a saving, I was resolved it should be of his own comfort, not mine.'

She went to bed, she said, 'in fear and trembling', but managed to sleep fairly well. 'On looking, however, at my fair hand in the morning, as it lay outside the bedclothes, I perceived it to be all—what shall I say?—elevated into inequalities. . . . Not a doubt of it, I had fallen among bugs!'

Old Sterling, immune, apparently, was perfectly content with his cheap lodging-house. 'Do you know,' Jane wrote to Carlyle, 'I pity this poor old man. The notion of saving seems to be growing into a disease with him.' The following night the bugs were more rampant than ever, 'having found,' said Jane, 'what a rare creature they had got to eat'; and Jane decided that she could stand it no longer. It was sad, for Ryde was 'certainly the most beautiful sea-bathing place I ever saw'. 'But what I get out of it for the time being, *moi*, is sleeplessness, indigestion, and incipient despair.'

On 12 August she fled back home. 'I have not for a long time enjoyed a more triumphant moment', she wrote, 'than in "descending" from the railway yesterday at Vauxhall, and calling for a porter to carry my small trunk and dressing box to a Chelsea steamer.' As she travelled up the Thames, she said, she consoled herself by thinking that in a few minutes she would be 'purified to the shift, to the very skin—should have absolutely *bathed* myself with *eau de Cologne*—should have some mutton broth set before me (I had written from Ryde to bespeak it!) and a silver spoon to eat it with (these four days had taught me to appreciate my luxuries), and the prospect of my own red bed at night! That of itself was enough to make me the most thankful woman in Chelsea!'

Helen opened the door to her, screaming with joy; and flinging her arms round her mistress's neck, kissed her 'from ear to ear'. Jane was truly thankful to be back; but Mazzini, who called that evening, was shocked by her appearance, declaring that she looked like 'Lady Macbeth in the sleeping scene'. Her sea-side holiday, far from benefiting her health, had exhausted her; but it had awakened in her a fresh enthusiasm for her home. Two good nights in her red bed set her up, 'and in token of my thankfulness to Providence,' she wrote to Carlyle, 'I fell immediately to glazing and painting with my own hands (not to ruin you altogether)'.

On 18 August Pearson and his men finished their work. The ladders, trestles, and all the paraphernalia that had spread itself over house and garden during the past six weeks were carried away, the floors swept clear of shavings and the stairs and hall washed clean of whitewash. The men shouldered their carpet-bags of tools, and for the last time the front door closed on the strains of 'Love's Young Dream' as the singing apprentice took himself off with his mates. Jane must have felt intense relief as she sat down in the quiet clean study to write to Carlyle. 'Both the public rooms,' she told him, were 'in a state of perfect habitableness' again, and now it only remained to clear up the bedrooms. She was longing, now, for Carlyle to come home, anxious for his approval of her 'clean pretty house', and of his own study particularly. Darwin, she wrote to her husband, ' "wondered if Carlyle would give admiration enough for all my needlework, etc. etc., feared not".' She proceeded to make a joke of Darwin's 'sarcastic sayings', but she clearly hoped that the hint would not pass unnoticed.

She was proud of the economy with which she had transformed his sparsely furnished workroom into 'a really beautiful little drawing room'. His books were arranged in the new shelves on either side of the fire, and over the chimney-piece hung a painting of Carlyle's mother. Portraits of her own family decorated the wall facing the windows, and 'you cannot think', she wrote to Jeannie

Welsh, 'how beautiful you . . . look on the pretty new wallpaper'. Her only purchase had been a new sofa; and that, as she told Carlyle, had cost him 'simply nothing at all'. She had had her eye on this sofa for a long time, but it was too dear, £4. 10*s*. The dealer had agreed to knock off £2 if she took it without mattress or cushions: but even £2. 10*s*. 'was more,' she said, 'than I cared to lay out of my own money on the article, so I did a stroke of trade with him. The old green curtains of downstairs were become filthy; and, what was better, superfluous. . . . So I sold them to the broker for thirty shillings; I do honestly think more than their value; but I higgled a full hour with him, and the sofa had lain on his hands. So you perceive,' she concluded triumphantly, 'there remained only one pound to pay.' Now, with a spare mattress of her own cut down to fit, and fresh cushions, the sofa was resplendent, like the rest of the furniture, in a cover of buff and red chintz made by Jane. Altogether, with his own bedroom newly carpeted and 'smartened up amazingly' she felt that the improvements could hardly fail 'to yield him "a certain" satisfaction, and obtain me some meed of praise'.

In mid-September Carlyle returned. He was bilious and out of sorts after the journey from Scotland. 'Blue pill with castor oil "and the usual trimmings",' said Jane, had to be resorted to immediately. But the house, she told Jeannie, 'was approved of as much as I had flattered myself it would be. And between ourselves,' she added, 'he would have been a monster if he had not exhibited some admiration more or less at my magnificent improvements achieved at so small a cost—to *him*.'

Carlyle wrote, years afterwards, of his 'mournful gratitude' for 'the fittings and re-fittings for me, full of loving ingenuity'. But alas, at this homecoming he was in no frame of mind to enjoy his surroundings. For four years he had been struggling with the idea of writing a book on Cromwell; reading endlessly, searching for facts, visiting the scenes of battles, growing increasingly irritable as time went by and still he could not begin to write, could not decide what form the book would take. 'Oh dear me,' said Jane, 'if all book writers took up the business as he does, fidgeting and flurrying about all the while like a hen in the distraction of laying its first egg . . . what a world of printed nonsense would be spared the long-suffering public!'

He came home from Scotland knowing that somehow he must force himself to set to work. His books of reference must be assembled and the piles of notes which had accumulated over the years; all his papers must be got out and sorted. After three days in the new study he was in a rage. 'There was no getting on in that upstairs room for want of a closet or some equivalent to fling one's confusion in.' 'Best to accumulate no confusion,' was Jane's tart retort. She was piqued, no doubt, by the reflection on her 'improvements' and refused to listen to Carlyle's argument that 'there must be a place for keeping all sorts of papers for a year or so, till one has made up one's mind what to burn and what not'.

Four days later the blow fell which was to destroy in half an hour all Jane's efforts of the past two months: one of the Miss Lamberts 'took a fit of playing' while Carlyle was at work. Evidently his long absence from home, and the din created by the workmen (for which Jane had written to apologize) had emboldened the young ladies to relax their former caution and fairly let themselves go on the instrument. The first outbreak was short-lived, and Jane tried to hope that it might not be repeated. Her hopes were dashed. Next morning again the piano tinkled gaily for another half-hour—'sufficient,' said Jane, 'to set all his nerves up for the rest of the day —and it was solemnly declared that "no life of Cromwell or any other book could ever be written alongside of that damnable noise".'

The *coup de grâce* was served by a cock, which crowed from a neighbouring garden and woke Carlyle at six for two mornings running. He now announced that his bedroom was uninhabitable. It was, said Jane wearily, 'just all the old eternal story commenced again'. Cheyne Row was unendurable, the noise could not be borne, he must get away to some solitude far from human habitation. 'Could one get a piece of ground to build some *crib* of a house upon at the Isle of Wight?' he demanded of Jane. Then, as reason intervened, he began to reconsider the possibilities of Cheyne Row. To escape from the noise he must have a room built on the roof: if he

were removed from them by two flights of stairs the Miss Lamberts
might play their accursed piano all day long and he would not hear
it. Jane must fetch Pearson the builder immediately for a consultation.

The cost of building a room at the top of the house 'silent as a
tomb, lighted from above' proved to be £120, and had to be aban-
doned; but Pearson was able to suggest methods of excluding noise
from Carlyle's bedroom. The shutters were to be stuffed with
cotton wool and kept tightly closed at night; and in order to
introduce a 'sufficiency of fresh air' zinc pipes were to be introduced
through the walls. Jane was sceptical. It was only because Carlyle
would sleep with the windows wide open that he heard this distant
cock; if he would try the simple expedient of shutting the window
and opening the door, the problem would be solved 'much more
cheaply than all this apparatus of stuffed shutters and zinc pipes'.

But Carlyle was in favour of stuffed shutters; the idea was worth
trying. So was another which occurred during his three-hour
consultation with Pearson. Until it became possible to build a study
at the top of the house, he would have to have one on the second
floor. His dressing-room, the small square closet leading out of his
bedroom, was the only possible place. It was small, certainly, only
7 feet square, but there was a good window, and room for his desk.
It was unheated: Pearson was prepared to put in a small fire-place
and 'break out' a chimney. While this work went on, Carlyle's
bedroom would be unusable; he agreed to move to the front of the
house, taking his stuffed shutters with him. Pearson suggested that
his temporary bedroom (formerly the spare room) would be immensely improved if a partition were taken down which divided it
from another much smaller room: it would then form one large,
handsome bedroom. This would be a simple job, done in a couple
of days, he said (in fact it took ten); and would be a great improvement to the house. Carlyle, determined now to carry out the
alterations without delay, gave orders for the work to proceed.

'So here', wrote Jane to Jeannie Welsh, 'is a quite other prospect
than that of quiet order which I was looking forward to for the
next twelve months at least! And I assure you it is with a heart-
rending sigh that I resign myself to the thought of lifting and

altering all the carpets again, . . . and having carpenters, plasterers
and whitewashers as before, besides the inconvenience of having
one's spare-room as it were annihilated—for could *you* for instance
sleep in a double-bedded room with Carlyle?'

Helen, faced with a fresh influx of workmen and all the attendant
mess and dirt, was 'struck with a temporary idiotcy', and Jane was
obliged, she said to follow her about and supply her with wits as
well as with active help at every turn. It was very disheartening
after all they had gone through that summer to see the house once
more turned upside down. Helen consoled herself with the thought,
'Well, if one's doing this, one's doing nothing else anyhow!'; but
Jane could not be so philosophic. This second earthquake was
infinitely worse than the first, for Carlyle was there in the middle
of it 'wringing his hands and tearing his hair, like the German
wizard servant who has learnt magic enough to make a broomstick
carry water for him, but had not the counter spell to stop it.
Myself,' she added wearily, 'could have sat down and cried.'

Carlyle, unable to sleep in his temporary bedroom, started
wandering about during the night: there were, said Jane, 'fires
kindled with his own hands, bread and butter eaten in the china
closet . . . and I all the while lying awake *listening* with a bouncing
heart but *afraid* to meddle with him. . . .'

The last straw was when Carlyle decided that the dining-room
grate could not be endured 'for another twenty-four hours—another
must be got—and then—as all our things are never to be made like
other people's but on some superior plan of our own—the new
grate—with rows of Dutch tiles—needed ever so much of the
chimney to be pulled down and a man building and plastering at it
for two days and a half'. That meant, of course, that all the carpets
and furniture of 'that beautifully clean room' had to be removed;
and in the meantime Jane had caught 'a fine rheumatism' in the back
of her neck from nailing down carpets upstairs. 'The hands of me,'
she told Jeannie, 'are absolutely blackened and coarsified.' She was
weary of the whole business. Once she had got that dining-room
carpet down again, and patched together a new one for the new
large spare room, she declared, she would get her hands cleaned

once and for all, put them into mitts, and 'lie on the sofa by heaven for two weeks and read French novels!'

It is unlikely that she fulfilled this ambition.

By the beginning of November the work was finished. Carlyle was installed in the new study which had been his dressing-room; and on 9 November he wrote to his mother: 'My little room here is such a curiosity as you have seldom seen; a place projecting off from my bedroom, about 7 or 8 feet square, papered on the walls, with a window in it which looks out upon gardens, trees and houses in the distance—and now with a fire-place, a shelf of books, my writing-table and a chair: here I sit, lifted above the noise of the world, *peremptory* to let no mortal enter my privacy here; and really I begin to like it'.

But only three days later Jane had been told the other side of the story. The new study was too small—'an abominable confined hole of a place'. Moreover there was no room in it for all the books he needed: 'one spends half one's time in running between it and the Library'. Then the wall-paper got on his nerves: it was 'a perfect solecism'. The room would need to be papered 'in some reasonable way,' he said, 'before one could feel it anything but the last refuge of a poor reduced beggar'.

In fact, the new study would not do. *Cromwell* was still hanging fire, tormenting him with problems. Trying to get started, he said, was 'like founding houses on bottomless quagmires; every stone when I have lugged it to the place is swallowed up in unknown depths of *gludder*'. He could not settle to work and he blamed his 'beggar's refuge'.

'And so,' said Jane, 'we move up and down thro' the house—trying ourselves there and then trying it here—and nowhere can any adjustment be effected. A sort of domestic *wandering Jew* he is become!'

And all on account of two heedless young women who could not resist playing the piano. Another carefully worded protest was pushed through the letter-box of number 6, which resulted in the Miss Lamberts '*trying*—with more or less success—to abstain from playing till two o'clock'. But the inconsiderate girls could not remain wholly silent. 'They seem tempted', wrote Jane, 'as often as they pass the seductive "instrument" to tinkle out of it a few "town-notes wild" or run over a scale or two just as if saying to themselves *"le bon temps viendra!"*'

Carlyle, lamenting the ruin of his large comfortable library, decided to follow up the protest with a gift, addressed to Miss Lambert, of his latest book, *Past and Present*. This was accompanied, Jane said, by 'a pretty letter of thanks for the attention she was showing to his wishes and an eloquent entreaty that she would go on with the same observance of the two o'clock system during his present labours'. This letter was worded, she said, with 'an insinuating poetry of expression sure to reach the heart of a plump young damsel like Miss Lambert'. She was right: an ecstatic reply assured Mr. Carlyle of her implicit observance of his request, and conveyed her 'love to Mrs. Carlyle'—a message which, as Jane observed, 'indicates a young lady still in the first enthusiasm of her faith in human nature'.

'And so,' said Jane, 'a gleam of hope has arisen for us.' Perhaps, after all the upheavals, the seemingly wasted alterations, the wanderings from room to room, *Cromwell* might in time come to be written, and in the study she had prepared with such loving trouble for its author.

*Cromwell* was written. After several false starts, the writing took less than two years: on 26 August 1845, Carlyle wrote 'I have this moment *ended* Oliver; hang it! He is ended, thrums and all.' During the next four years the book went through three editions.

By the beginning of 1850 Carlyle was writing his *Latter Day Pamphlets* and the following January he began what was for him a labour of love. His friend John Sterling had died of tuberculosis in 1844; 'I am throwing down on paper some account of J. Sterling's life', he wrote in March 1851. The book was published in November and had a considerable success. 'None of Mr. Cs'. Books have sold with such rapidity as this one', Jane wrote to John Carlyle. 'If he would write a *Novel* we should become as rich as—Dickens!'

But Carlyle, free to contemplate a new subject, was re-reading German history: Preuss's *Friedrich* fired him with the idea of writing on Frederick the Great and his battles. 'I am taking more and more to my German historical studies', he wrote in April 1852, and by June he was 'reading about the Seven Years' war with ten maps spread out before me', and planning a visit to Germany. Not yet aware of the gargantuan task that lay ahead, he was becoming immersed in his subject; he must go to Germany, he and Jane must both go to Germany: they must spend a year there.

Jane was appalled. 'For a little while well and good—but for a whole year to have nothing to fall back upon under his and my own *gloom*!' she wrote to Helen Welsh. But at this juncture a situation arose which gave her a good excuse to stay at home.

In June 1852 a new lease was signed between Alfred Oldridge (a new landlord) and Thomas Carlyle, by which the Carlyles obtained tenancy of the house for thirty-one years. The rent of £35 was not raised 'in consideration of the permanent improvement to be effected to the property by the carrying out of' alterations and repairs suggested by the tenants.

These alterations and repairs were considerable, and were to be put in hand at once. The builder's specifications were submitted and approved; and the work, it was promised, would take six weeks.

On 5 July 1852, Jane undertook what proved to be the longest and most expensive earthquake of all, which was not to end for over a year, and which was to culminate in the building of the long-dreamt-of Silent Room.

CHAPTER SIX

# The Soundproof Study

I T seemed that at last Carlyle had resolved to settle down and
make the best of Cheyne Row. He was prepared to lay out money
on improving and modernizing the house. 'We have got a lease of
31 years', he wrote to his brother John in July 1852, 'and a fair basis
for changing the house into our own image as nearly as it will come:
so *en avant*! The place too is very cheap:\* and on the present terms
(whatever become of *us*) an outlay of £200 or £250 is considered a
perfectly safe investment.'

The voice of Jane can be heard behind this statement. For a
couple of weeks she had been active, 'running up and down to the
City and elsewhere—after the *lease* and the lawyers, and house-
agents and architects and the devil knows what'—and now the plan,

---

\*The rent was still £35 a year.

presented as a *fait accompli*, was accepted by Carlyle, and her one anxiety was to get him out of the house before the work started.

It would be an upheaval. Water was to be laid on from the water-works, and two cisterns, one at the top of the house and one in the kitchen, would supply a tap over the kitchen sink with running water. Gaslight was to be introduced; but only two jets were contemplated, one over the front door and one in the kitchen. Gas was expensive, and the flickering batswing burner did not give as good a light for reading as an oil lamp; but it was practical in the kitchen where lamps and candles were easily knocked over.

But the most ambitious project, at this stage, was the improvement of Carlyle's library—'an enlargement of it into a kind of Drawing Room according to modern ideas', as he put it. He still did most of his work in this room, the Miss Lamberts and their piano being now a thing of the past, but he seems to have been prepared to hand over his workroom in the evenings to the demands of sociability. The library was clearly the only room where parties could be held; and the Carlyles were now in a position where they must, however modestly, entertain. Not only were they constantly visited by a growing circle of writers and artists, but they were mixing in Society.

In July 1851 Jane wrote to Mrs. Russell, 'I never went to so many fine parties and bothered so much about *dresses*, etc. . . . as this summer!' 'Mr. C.', she continues, 'having no longer such a dislike to great parties as he once had, I fall naturally into the current of London life—and a very *fast* one it is!'

There was no doubt about it: Mr. C.—though his digestion suffered from indiscreet experiments with rich food—was taking a sort of pleasure in being a literary lion. It was not only Lady Ashburton who sought his company at her soirées. 'Lady Derby (the Premier's wife) intends, it would appear, a great turn out . . . on the last evening of the month, and has sent me a card', he writes to his sister Jean. 'I shall go for a few minutes, and see what the "scoonerils"* are like!'

In spite of his deep-rooted prejudice against 'gigmanity' Carlyle

*Scoundrels (Annandale Scots).

enjoyed the opportunity to study the people who wielded power. Through the Ashburtons he met Sir Robert Peel, whom he had always admired; the admiration was reciprocated, and Carlyle dined at Peel's house in May 1850. A month later both Carlyles went to a Ball at Bath House where they encountered 'from five to seven hundred select aristocracy'. 'By far the most interesting figure present', wrote Carlyle, 'was the old Duke of Wellington.' He was struck by the 'expression of graceful simplicity, veracity and nobleness there is about the old hero when you see him close at hand'. But Palmerston, whom he met at a soirée given by Mr. and Mrs. Monckton Milnes, impressed him less favourably. '. . . Small bloodshot cruel eyes—otherwise a tall man, with some air of greediness and cunning; and a curious fixed *smile* as if lying not at the top but at the bottom of his physiognomy.'

In 1851 Mrs. Carlyle went to stay at Alderley Park with Lord and Lady Stanley. Their daughter Blanche, who had taken a great fancy to Jane, was about to be married to Lord Airlie. Jane was amused by the young bride's attitude. 'Poor Blanche doesn't seem to know, amidst the excitement and rapture of the *trousseau*, whether she loves the *man* or not—she hopes well enough at least for practical purposes!'

Perhaps a note of pride may be detected in some of Jane's references to noble friends—'A young friend of mine married the Earl of Airlie last autumn, and asks me to visit her at Cortachy Castle', she wrote to Mrs. Russell three months later—but she never lost her clear judgement of people on their own merits. She was obliged to entertain more, and grander, guests, and she was an excellent hostess; but it was only 'a small tea-party' to which Lady Stanley was invited in April 1852. The Carlyles' simple way of living remained unaltered, and so did Jane's housekeeping money until, in 1853, rising prices obliged her to ask for £30 a year more.

But it was with a sense of increased social obligations that, in the summer of 1851, they decided to improve the house.

Jane's bedroom was to be sacrificed. Three feet were to be cut off and added to the drawing-room, giving it a depth of over 17 feet.

More space could also be provided, it was found, by taking away the old-fashioned fire-place and chimney-breast ('*two feet* of that great tower of brickwork', wrote Carlyle) and replacing it with a modern Bramah grate set nearer to the wall. The three window frames were to be lengthened, and the Queen Anne windows with their heavy wooden bars and smallish oblong panes replaced by 'new proper windows with a great increase of light'—the lower sashes to be glazed with ground glass. The reason for this last is obscure; probably the idea was to combine light with privacy from the street. There were also to be new shutters, and Venetian blinds to shade the room on summer afternoons.

The old panelling was now to be completely removed; and the walls plastered and papered, with a plaster cornice. The floor round the fire-place would have to be relaid, and also the floor of the bedroom above, where the chimney-breast had to be cut back to correspond with the new drawing-room chimney below.

The panelling of the hall and staircase was to be papered over, and painted and grained to look like mahogany.

On 5 July 1852—just nine years after the last major earthquake— the house was once again invaded. Pearson, the Church Street builder, had not been invited to do the work this time, but a man called Morgan (*not* of Pope's Head Alley); and it was Morgan's 'legion of devils', armed with all the old familiar impedimenta, who rushed in early that morning and spread themselves over the house. The work began in a heatwave—'the thermometer standing at 83 in the shade'; and after a day or two Jane began to realize that the builder's promise to finish in six weeks was wildly optimistic. The workmen, she told Mrs. Russell, 'spend three fourths of their time in consulting how the work should be done, and in going out and in after "beer" . . . and then a thorough repair complicated by the alteration of chimneys and partitions, and by heat at 82 in the shade, was a wild piece of work with any sort of workmen. The builder promised to have all done in six weeks, painting included; if he gets done in six months is as much as I hope.'

And meanwhile, to make things worse, 'Mr. C., exactly at the wrong moment, has been seized with an invincible disposition to *stay where he is.*' This upset all her plans. 'Why Mr. Carlyle, who is anything rather than needed, stays on I can't imagine.' She unburdened herself to Mrs. Russell and to Helen Welsh: 'If Mr. C. had but gone away, I should have had *his* bedroom, which is only to be papered and painted; into which I might have stowed myself and the furniture for a time—but he has had the little dressing-room turned into a most delectable study for the occasion, and there he sits serene in the middle of a noise as of the battle of Waterloo, and universal chaos throughout the rest of the house—and then of course *meals* and all that sort of thing must go on as usual, and cold baths!'

To add to her distresses, she was servantless, the last maid, Ann, having fallen ill and left just before the earthquake. A local child, Martha, who had been helping during Ann's illness, had to be fetched back to attend to Carlyle's wants and give a hand with the meals.

Meanwhile, Carlyle was writing serenely to his brother John, 'I am banished up to my little dressing-closet here, behind the bedroom; here stands my desk, with a few books . . .' The heat, he says, 'is not quite so unendurable as I expected; I have off all the carpets here; I keep a watering-pot beside me, and fearlessly moisten both floors and walls; so that with windows down, and plenty of wind blowing, and almost no clothes at all, I contrive to get along'.

But by the end of two weeks, heat, noise and lack of sleep had had their effect, and on 22 July he went off to Scotland. He was evidently in a frenzy of nerves when he left home: Jane went by boat with him to the docks and saw him off on the steamer; and two days later she wrote:

'Oh my! I wonder if I shall hear tomorrow morning, and what I shall hear! Perhaps that somebody drove you wild with snoring, and that you killed him and threw him into the sea! Had the boatmen upset the boat on the way back, and drowned little Nero and me, on purpose, I could hardly have taken it ill of them, seeing they "were but men, of like passions with yourself".'

The night after Carlyle's departure she 'went to bed at eleven, fell asleep at three, and rose at six. The two plumbers were rushing about the kitchen with boiling lead; an additional carpenter was waiting for my directions about the cupboard at the bottom of the kitchen stair. The two usual carpenters were hammering at the floor and windows of the drawing room. The bricklayer rushed in, in plain clothes, measured the windows for stone sills, rushed out again, and came no more that day.' 'After breakfast,' she told her husband, I fell to clearing out the front bedroom for the bricklayers, removing everything into your room. When I had just finished, a wild-looking stranger, with a paper cap, rushed up the stairs, three steps at a time, and told me he was "sent by Mr. Morgan to get on with the painting of Mr. Carlyle's bedroom during his absence!" I was so taken by surprise that I did not feel at first to have any choice in the matter. . . . Then I came in mind that the windows and doors had to be repaired, and a little later that the floor was to be taken up!' Clearly Mr. C.'s room could not yet be painted but; 'being desirous not to refuse the good the gods had provided', she told the man he could paint her bedroom instead, and set about moving out all her furniture. 'I next cleared myself a road into your bedroom,' she told Carlyle, 'and fell to moving all the things of mine up there also. Certainly no lady in London did such a hard day's work. . . . I never went out till ten at night, when I took a turn or two on Battersea Bridge, without having my throat cut.' Her letter ends reassuringly: 'I don't mind the uproar a bit now that you are out of it.'

After two or three bad nights she began to settle down and enjoy herself. Now that Carlyle was out of the way, she told his brother John, 'and I feel the dirt and disorder with my own senses, and not through his as well, it is amazing how little I care about it. Nay, in superintending all these men I begin to find myself "in the career open to my particular talents", and am infinitely more satisfied than I was in talking "*wits*" in my white silk gown with feathers on my head, and *soirées* at Bath House, and all that sort of thing. It *is* a consolation to be of some *use*, tho' it were only in helping stupid carpenters and bricklayers out of their "impossibilities" . . . and when Mr. C. is not here recognising it with his overwhelming eloquence, I can regard the present earthquake as something almost *laughable*.'

At this juncture Jane endured yet another servant crisis. The night before Carlyle went away a new maid had arrived. She was, wrote Jane, 'a great beauty, whom I engaged because she had been six years in her last place'—and because Carlyle had 'decidedly liked her physiognomy'. Unfortunately this young woman, finding the household in chaos and 'unable', as Jane put it, 'to recover from the bewilderment of the scene in which she found herself', filled in her time listening at keyholes and reading her mistress's letters. Her curiosity was insatiable. 'In every little box, drawer, and corner,' said Jane, 'I found traces of her prying. It was going to be like living under an Austrian Spy.' Jane quickly made up her mind: the Beauty, as she called her, would have to go. Fortunately the Beauty made things easy for her by giving notice. The place, she said, didn't suit her—'it was such a muddle, and would be such a muddle for months to come, that she thought it best to get out of it'.

'I was never more thankful for a small mercy in all my life', wrote Jane after the door had closed on the departing treasure. 'Our Beauty was as perfect a fool as the sun ever shone on', she told Carlyle. She felt she was in luck, for on the very same day a girl who had worked for her before, known as Irish Fanny, arrived at tea-time, 'to tell me she had left her place. I offered her mine, which she had already made trial of, and she accepted with an enthusiasm which did one's heart good after all these cold, ungrateful English wretches.'

Fanny was to come in a month's time; and meanwhile Martha was asked to remain, as stopgap. 'Little Martha is gone to bed the happiest child in Chelsea at the honour done her,' said Jane. She had taken a fancy to this little cockney, and tried to get her a situation in a larger household. 'I have the dearest little girl of fifteen—wanting a *place*', she wrote to Kate Sterling on 25 July. 'She reads beautifully and writes beautifully and sews beautifully—has the most *soothing* manners, and the most upright disposition. Should you want any such creature, tell me. I should like you to have her.' Unfortunately, history doesn't relate what did become of little

Martha; but as she sewed so beautifully and had such soothing manners she may well have been a success, ending up as lady's maid, as a reward for her upright disposition.

At the beginning of August Jane packed her night-things into a bag, and taking her dog, Nero, in a basket, went off to spend two nights with the Macreadys at Sherborne. It seems a long way to have gone for only two nights; but Mrs. Macready was hopelessly ill and not expected to live. The visit was a sad one, but the change, and the complicated adventurous journeys did Jane good, and she returned to Cheyne Row with renewed energy. She was impatient at the slow progress the men were making. 'My dear, my prophetic gift says very decidedly that it will be two months at least before we get these fearful creatures we have conjured up *laid*', she wrote to Carlyle. 'The confusion at this moment is more horrible than when you went away.' The worst of all was that Mr. Morgan, the *deus ex machina*, never came, never could be got at. She tackled one of the workmen, 'a dashing young man', who told her calmly, 'My dear madam, you must have patience, indeed you must; it will all be done—some day!'

A week later she was more optimistic; she was anxious that Carlyle should not fret about the house or her discomfort. 'For my part, I am got quite used to the disturbance, and begin to like the— what shall I say?—excitement of it.' She had begun once more to enjoy the drama, of which she herself was heroine—even though, at times, it seemed more tragic than comic.

'It were well worth your while to drive up from Headley just to take a look at this house', she wrote to Kate Sterling. 'Everything getting torn down and nothing getting put up, and the furniture gathering itself (oh if it would but gather *itself*!) into larger and more chaotic heaps, as more flooring is lifted and more chimneys pulled down; more and wilder men turned loose on the premises . . . and no composure nor help nor hope but in my own head and hands, to keep me from being swallowed up in the general mess!' She becomes more dramatic as the subject gets hold of her: 'To have no regular bed to sleep in, and to dress with two carpenters in your room, and to be constantly powdered with lime and choked with dust, all that is no joke! And I can't get out of it, at least England expects of me to remain, for it is my "duty".'

Fortunately, it was lovely weather—fine and sunny, but cooler, with temperatures in the 70's. She had taken refuge in the front dining-room, which was the only place free of workmen. Here she managed to preserve some degree of order. The room was separated by a screen from the back dining-room, which was being used as a dumping-ground, and 'the bedding, and tables with legs in the air, as if in convulsions, which show themselves above the screen, often make me laugh'. When the noise from upstairs was very great, she told her husband, she practised on the piano. 'I do quite well, in short; and don't see how I can be spared till things are done to my mind, and the chaotic heaps of furniture restored to their proper places.'

Meals were a problem, with no regular servant, and workmen in and out of the kitchen. (Among other things, a new range was being installed.) 'Meat dinners at home,' Jane declared, 'are as nearly impossible as can be, and one sleeps ill on tea-dinners.' So she went to Verrey's in Regent Street, and dined off a mutton chop and a glass of bitter ale. 'The charge at Verey's [*sic*] is very moderate, and the cooking perfect. For my dinner and ale today I paid one-and-fivepence.' Another day she dined 'at a clean-looking shop in the Strand', where she had half a roast chicken, a large slice of ham and three new potatoes for a shilling. She enjoyed these expeditions, which were unconventional, to say the least, but Jane did not care. 'I am beyond such considerations at present.' Besides, she assured Carlyle, she was not the only woman dining alone at Verrey's; she had seen others—'not improper—governesses and the like'.

She made light of her discomforts to Carlyle; she was determined that he should remain away while she herself felt impelled to stay at home. There had been talk of their both going to Germany: now she urged him to go without her, assuring him that she had no wish to go herself at present. 'I don't take it the least unkind you leaving me behind; and with Neuberg to attend on you, I really think you would be better without me', she wrote on 3 August. Three days later she pursued the subject. 'But of Germany: I really would advise you to go—not so much for the good of *doing it,* but for the good of having *done it.* . . . And I also vote for leaving me out of the question. It would be anything but a *pleasure* for me to be there, with the notion of a house all at sixes and sevens to come home to. . . . You will take me there another time if you think it worth my seeing.' She goes on to reassure Carlyle on the progress of the earthquake. The men, she now sees, are doing well, taking more trouble over the whole thing than she had realized. 'There is an immense deal of invisible work expended on it which you expended on *Cromwell.* The two carpenters are not *quick,* certainly, but they are very conscientious and assiduous, giving themselves a great deal of work that makes no show, but which you should be the last man to count unnecessary.'

At the beginning of September the painters moved in. The house was still desperately uncomfortable, and she was thankful that Carlyle had at last taken her advice and sailed (on 29 August) from Leith to Rotterdam, on his way to Bonn. For a week, with the reek of paint in her nostrils, Jane alternated between sleeping on the dining-room sofa and a bed she had hired at number 2 Cheyne Walk, which had to be given up in a hurry when it was found to be infested with bugs. She gratefully accepted an invitation from Lady Ashburton to spend three nights at Addiscombe—'being very anxious to have a Christian bed for a night or two'; but alas, the Christian bed was 'entirely curtainless' and she got no more sleep there, she said, 'than among the bugs at number 2'.

By this time the new servant, Fanny, had arrived and installed herself in the back kitchen—the front kitchen being still in a state of chaos. Fanny was Irish and happy-go-lucky; she made light of the muddle, and was a great comfort to her mistress. After her visit to Addiscombe, Jane came home to a thunderstorm, and crawled, exhausted, into the only available bed, which was Carlyle's, in a newly-painted room, carpetless and piled with lumber. The paint smell gave her colic and a violent headache, and she spent all the next day prostrate on the dining-room sofa, 'in desperate agony, with a noise going on around me like the crack of doom'. 'If it had not been for Fanny's kindness,' she told Carlyle, 'who, when all else failed, fairly took to crying and sobbing over me, I think I must have died of the very horror and desolation of the thing; for the plasterers came back yesterday to finish the cornice in the new room, and the bricklayers were tramping out and in repairing the backyard; and the painter was making a rare smell of new paint in my old bedroom; besides the two carpenters, into whose head the devil put it to saw the whole day, at God knows what, without a moment's intermission, except to hammer. I have passed a good many bad days in this world,' she concludes, 'but never one so utterly wretched from mere physical and material causes.'

Fanny, she told Carlyle, was the greatest blessing, 'so willing to fly over the moon for me, and always making light of her discomforts'. Fanny must indeed have been uncomfortable, crushed into the back kitchen, with no proper bed, and only an open fire with two trivets to cook upon.

A day or two later Jane had quite recovered, was running into the city on business, and holding an evening tea-party in the front dining-room. 'There were six of us,' she said, 'and we spoke four languages.' (She was entertaining a rich Russian exile who had helped Mazzini: an Italian, Saffi, was invited to meet him, also the Graf von Reichenbach and his wife, and Erasmus Darwin. The four languages were, presumably, French, German, Italian, and English.) Fanny, who served the tea, was still in high favour: 'really a nice servant; a dash of Irish "rough and ready" in her but a good cleaner, and a good cook, and a perfect incarnation of "The Willing mind". Very tidy too in her own person in all circumstances.'

Fanny's good nature was put to another test when, the front kitchen being at last finished, she prepared to move in, and 'fell to taking the bed to pieces to give it a good washing'. She found that it was infested with bugs.

The old four-posted wooden bed had probably never completely recovered from Helen. The last maid, Ann, ordered to take it down before she left, said blandly that she had found 'nothing worth mentioning—just four bugs, and those very small ones'. 'Like the girl's illegitimate child,' commented Jane.

Ann's report had been an understatement. The bed, said Jane, 'perfectly swarmed' with bugs, was impregnated with them beyond even her cleansing powers. Most people would have burnt the whole thing forthwith; but not Jane.

'We gathered it all up, and carried it out into the garden to be sold to a broker, who is coming for certain rubbish of things.' 'I went the same day,' she added, 'and bought a little iron bedstead for the kitchen, for one pound two-and-sixpence.'

A few weeks later Fanny was sound asleep in this little iron bedstead when thieves climbed through the larder window and made their way into the back kitchen. Fanny, 'though not conscious of having heard them', woke suddenly, stretched out her hand for a handkerchief, and knocked over a brass candlestick, which made, she said, 'a devil of a row'. This disturbed the men, who—baffled by the bolts on the back kitchen door—beat a hurried retreat the way they came. Fanny was alone in the house.

Jane, who had been 'chased from room to room by the smell of paint', had finally taken refuge in a lodging-house in Hemus Street, the other side of the King's Road. On the night of the burglary she slept badly. Rising early with a bad headache, she made her way home through pours of rain, 'thinking resolutely of the hot coffee that Fanny would have all ready for me, to be taken at the kitchen fire, and the kind sympathy that she would accompany it with. On reaching my own door', she wrote to John Carlyle. 'I could hardly stand, and leant on the rails till it was opened.'

But the door was opened not by kind Fanny but by Mrs. Heywood—'a decent, disagreeable young woman' who had been giving a hand with the cleaning.

' "Oh," she said, the first thing, "we are glad you are come! Fanny is in such a way! The house has been broken into during the night! the police are now in the kitchen!" '

'Here was a cure for a sick headache!' said Jane. Wet, faint, dizzy with pain, she made her way down to the kitchen, where stood two police sergeants, 'writing down in a book the stolen items from Fanny's dictation; she, poor thing, looking deathly. There was no coffee, of course—no fire even. . . .'

Jane's headache was forgotten. She was filled with indignation against Morgan the builder. He was to blame for this disaster. Already he was in her black books. 'I have ceased to write to him, or send any messages to him. I merely pray to God to "very particularly damn him" ', she had written on 25 September. Now he had left the larder window without a frame for three weeks—a positive invitation to thieves. Had it not been for the bolts on the outside of the back kitchen door, the whole house would have been robbed.

As it was, it was Fanny who suffered the greatest loss. Her 'nice new large trunk' had been in the back kitchen; the men had broken off the lock, and 'tumbled all the contents on the floor, carrying away two shawls, two new dresses, and a variety of articles', but fortunately overlooking Fanny's savings—three sovereigns wrapped in brown paper and hidden at the bottom of her box. One of Jane's silver spoons had been left about, and this was taken, together with 'a tablecloth (good), which had been drying Nero'. The men ate a home-made cake and drank the milk left out for Jane's breakfast, and 'left dirty prints of naked feet all over the larder shelf, on which they stepped from the window'. They had also burnt a hole in the new shelf, where they had left a lighted candle burning. 'A mercy,' said Jane, 'the fine new house was not set on fire!'

Fanny was remunerated: her loss, Jane reckoned, amounted to 'four sovereigns . . . which, of course, I gave her, though she was not expecting, poor thing, to be compensated, and kept declaring she was thankful it was her, and not the mistress, that had lost most'.

But she was in a great state of nerves, and Mr. Piper the postman offered to come and sleep in the house; but Jane declined his offer and gave up her room in Hemus Street. She felt it her duty to keep Fanny company; moreover, Mrs. Piper had told her that her husband 'would be quite useless against thieves, as he slept like a stone'.

Jane had iron bars fixed into the larder window 'independently of Mr. Morgan', and went to bed with a pair of loaded pistols beside her. 'I took care,' she said, 'to let all the workmen and extraneous people about, know of my loaded pistols. The painter came and examined them one day when I was out, and said to Fanny: "I shouldn't like to be a thief within twenty feet of your mistress, with one of these pistols in her hand. I shouldn't give much for my life; she has such a devil of a straight eye!" '

She recounted this to John Carlyle. To her husband, still in Germany, all she said, two days after the burglary, was 'I had to give up my snug little lodging suddenly and remain here, for "reasons which it may be interesting not to state".' She preferred not to tell Carlyle, she explained to Doctor John, 'in case he should take it into his head to be uneasy, which is not likely, but just possible'.

For three days after the robbery, 'policemen, four of them, kept coming in plain clothes, and in uniform . . . talking the most confounded nonsense, and then died away *re infecta*'. And the thieves were not caught. There were other signs of their activies. Mr. Chalmers, the Carlyles' neighbour at number 4, 'had a pair of heavy steps carried over his wall, and applied to the window of number 1 the same night, and a pair of bad worsted stockings left in his conservatory. . . . The window at number 1 was got up a little way, but stuck there. Almost every night since,' wrote Jane a fortnight after the robbery, 'some house has been entered or attempted, and still the police go about 'with their fingers in their mouths".'

She continued to sleep with her pistols beside her, and woke at the smallest noise. One night, 'alarmed by a sound as of a pane of glass cut', she 'leapt out of bed and struck a light, and listened'. The sound was repeated, followed by 'a great bang, like the breaking in of some panel. I took my loaded pistols', Jane wrote to Mrs. Russell, 'and went downstairs.' There was another bang, which she perceived was from outside the front door.

' "What do you want?" I asked; "who are you?" "It's the policeman, if you please; do you know that your parlour windows are both open?" It was true! I had forgotten to close them, and the policeman had first tried the bell, which made the shivering sound, the wire being detached from the bell, and when he found he could not ring it he had beaten on the door with his stick, the knocker also being off while it was getting painted. I could not help laughing,' she adds, 'at what the man's feelings would have been had he known of the cocked pistol within a few inches of him.'

Meanwhile, the earthquake rumbled on. Jane was disgusted with

Morgan's slackness. It was October, and there was no sign of the work being finished. 'All the thoughts of my heart just now are curses on Mr. Morgan', she wrote to Carlyle. 'Never in my life has my temper been so tried. So anxious I have been to get on, and the workmen only sent here, seemingly, when they have nowhere else to go, and Mr. Morgan dwindled away into a myth! Not once have I seen his face!' Carlyle was talking of coming home. 'I will have your bedroom at least in order for you,' she promised him.

She decided that the new drawing-room would have to remain unpapered till the spring, and the dining-room would have to do without new paint. Instead she set Fanny and Mrs. Heywood to wash the woodwork, and cleaned the wall-paper herself. All three of them then set to, polishing up the furniture which had been dumped for so long, and restoring it 'to its old condition'.

The new big drawing-room, she told Carlyle, was clean and habitable, 'though sufficiently bare-looking'. 'When it is papered and furnished prettily,' she went on, 'it will be a very fine room indeed.' Mr. Chalmers, their wealthy neighbour, a great 'improver' himself, had been invited to look at it. He said, wrote Jane, 'with a look of envy, that we couldn't have got a house with such a room in it under a hundred and fifty pounds a year'. This was some consolation for the trials she had endured.

Towards the end of October, Carlyle came home—'half dead, out of those German horrors of indigestion, insomnia, and continual chaotic wretchedness,' as he put it. It can hardly have been a joyous homecoming. He found, he wrote in his Journal, 'seas of paint still flooding everything, and my poor Jane so beaten in her hard battle—a wild hard battle in many ways, and in which I cannot help thee, poor kind vehement soul for ever dear to me'.

Carlyle was in no frame of mind to endure the discomfort at Cheyne Row, so Jane and he accepted Lady Ashburton's invitation to stay at The Grange for the time being. After a week or two Jane came home to see the last of the workmen and get things ready for her husband's return; and when he arrived she 'had the place clear of workers at last, clean as her wont is, and shining with gas at the door, and other lights to welcome me to tea'.

This time Thomas was in a better mood to appreciate his improved home.

'The house is clearly very much bettered; this room of mine in particular' (the new drawing-room-library) 'and my bedroom upstairs, are, or will be, perfect beauties of rooms in their way', he wrote to his mother. 'I am terribly *brashed*', he continued, 'with all these tumblings about, and have not yet fairly recovered my feet, but with quiet, with pious endeavour, I shall surely do so . . . and on the whole, I hope to get to a little *work* again, and that is the consolation which surpasses all for me.'

*Frederick* had been in Carlyle's mind for two years now—'and much reading and considering going on; but even yet, after my German investments of toil and pain, I felt uncertain, disinclined. . . .'

He could not get started. On 5 December he wrote, 'As usual many things, or almost all things, are conspiring to hinder me from any clear work, or to choke up my power of working altogether.' He was beset by all the old familiar devils: indigestion, sleeplessness, intense depression—and noise. On 12 November he had taken up his pen and written the following:

'To G. Remington, 6 Cheyne Row.

'Dear Sir,—It is with great reluctance that I venture to trouble you in any way; but a kind of necessity compels me; and I trust your good nature will excuse it in a distressed neighbour.

'We have the misfortune to be people of weak health in this house; bad sleepers in particular; and exceedingly sensible in the night hours to disturbances from sound. On your premises for some time past there is a Cock. . . .

'If you would have the goodness to remove that small animal or in any way render him inaudible from midnight to breakfast time, such charity would work a notable relief to certain persons here, and be acknowledged by them as an act of good neighbourship.

'With many apologies, and neighbourly respects,

'I remain, Yours sincerely,

T. Carlyle.'

The letter received a polite acknowledgement, the 'small animal' was promptly silenced, but Carlyle's problems were not solved.

' "*Frederick the Great*" continues very questionable', he told his sister on 23 December. In March 1853 he wrote, 'I begin to *try* more seriously to get something gradually brought to paper'; on 13 April he was 'still struggling and haggling about Frederick': but in May he was complaining of 'the want of sufficient *love* for lean Frederick and his heroisms, on my part—which is a sad objection indeed!'

And as Carlyle wrestled, Jane was writing, 'Cocks are springing up more and more, till it seems as if the Universe were growing into one poultry yard . . . All that has waked up Mr. C. into the old phrenzy to be "off into silence"!'

Cocks were not the only disturbers of the peace. Cheyne Row, on to which his library windows looked, had become a busy street along which horses and carts rattled continually and street vendors shouted their wares. Organ-grinders—'vile yellow Italians'— ground out their raucous music under his open windows and had to be paid to go away; and in the summer evenings the fireworks at Cremorne distracted him with their bangings and splutterings and the ecstatic cries of the spectators.

He had determined to take no holiday. In July, Jane, who was thin and tired, agreed to go to Scotland: Carlyle remained at Cheyne Row. There had been more talk of a 'silent room'; for the present, however, the great expense of last year's earthquake, and his reluctance to face yet another upheaval decided him to try and make the best of things.

But soon it became clear that if 'Frederick' were to be written he would have to find quiet somehow. In the summer, with windows open, the house was intolerable. Polite Mr. Remington had left number 6, and the rumbustious Roncas had moved in, and were beginning to make themselves felt. With no Jane to intervene, 'the unprotected male' grew desperate. 'I foresee in general these cocks will require to be abolished, entirely silenced', he wrote to Jane, 'whether we build the new room or not. I would cheerfully shoot them, and pay the price if discovered, but I have no gun. . . .' 'The cocks must either withdraw or die!' he wrote two days later. He was in despair. 'Being now fairly in for Frederick', he wrote after-wards, 'and the poultry, parrots, Cochin China, and vermin like to drive one mad, I at last gave in.' He determined to put in hand the long-discussed plan for a soundproof room at the top of the house.

Jane wrote encouraging him. 'I am decidedly of the opinion that one should make oneself independent of Ronca and all contingencies by building the "sound-proof" room, since so much money has already been spent on that house.'

On 11 August Carlyle wrote to his sister Mrs. Aitken:

'All summer I have been more or less annoyed with *noises*, even accidental ones, which get free access through my open windows: all the tinkering and "repairing" has done no good in that respect. . . . At length, after deep deliberation, I have fairly decided to have a top storey put upon the house, one big apartment, 20 feet square, with thin *double* walls, light from the top, etc., and artfully ventilated—into which no sound *can* come; and all the cocks in nature may crow round it, without my hearing a whisper of them!'

Once the decision was made, he lost no time putting it into effect. In his Journal for 17 August he wrote, 'Masons are upon the roof of the house, after a dreadful bout of resolution on my part, building me a soundless room. The world, which can do me no good, shall at least not torment me with its street and backyard noises.'

The project, suggested originally by 'an ingenious needy builder', was taken up enthusiastically by a friend and admirer of Carlyle's, John Chorley, who promptly constituted himself architect and, as Jane put it, 'over-ruling Providence of the whole thing'. Chorley, 'once a gentleman of mark in the Railway world and elsewhere' (wrote Carlyle), 'at present, a retired philosopher, tho' still young; really a clever learned man, and very fond of *me*', was also 'the only person now known to me in the world who fairly possesses the faculty of *mending a pen*'. Making him the gift of a double-bladed knife with a buckhorn handle, Carlyle gratefully handed over to Chorley the planning of his new attic study.

Chorley consulted Cubitt's, who 'agreed to send a "*right man*" '. Estimates were tendered, and specifications submitted, to which Chorley added his own notes and suggestions.

The plan was, in fact, 'to take off the present roof and build a new room; put on a new curb roof with a proper skylight made to open, and of suitable dimensions for the size of the room. Prepare and put up a pair of horizontal glazed sashes to run easily on brass rollers under the skylight, forming an air chamber between. The roof to be boarded and covered with the best Bangor slate. Form an air chamber between slating and the whole surface of the room.'

Double walls were to be built at the east and west end of the room (that is, the back and front of the house), forming on each side a cupboard about 3 feet deep between inner and outer wall. These cupboards were to be furnished with 'small double windows' for light and ventilation 'if required'.

The specification also provided for a stove, 'and air flues with proper ventilators on the side opposite the fireplace'. ('And two on the side of the stove', added John Chorley.) There were to be ventilators in the skirting, and under the roof.

A new staircase had to be built, with balustrading copied from the existing stairs below. The cistern, put in the year before, was to be moved up under the new roof, and a lead-lined sink with running water fixed on the landing where the cistern had stood.

The study was to be given 'a good floor of $\frac{7}{8}$ in. yellow pine'; large deal cupboards fitted with shelves were to be built in the north-east corner of the room, and all the woodwork was to be painted and grained. The walls were to be covered with a good paper, 'as may be chosen' ('by Mr. Carlyle', wrote John Chorley, adding 'The Builder also to fix a suitable bell with handle in the room').

The work, it was estimated, would take six weeks, and cost £169.

But when Jane came home at the beginning of September little had been done: there was a strike among the builders' men, and Irish labourers were brought in. At last the work started, it being agreed that everything was to be done from outside the house. 'The workpeople', Jane wrote to Kate Sterling, 'go up the outside of the house by ladders thank God—and won't come in, they promise, till the new stairs have to be made.' Her opinion of Chorley as architect was tinged with contempt. 'It is a fine time for John Chorley, who . . . is to be seen running up and down the long ladder in front of the house the first thing of a morning when one looks abroad.'

In spite of Chorley's efforts to protect Carlyle, the house was soon 'in a crisis of discomfort', as Jane put it. The Irish labourers proved unworthy of their hire. Disasters began to occur. 'One Irish Artist,' said Carlyle, '. . . ignorant that lath and plaster was not a floor . . . came plunging down into my bedroom, catching himself by the armpits, fast swinging, astonished in the vortex of old laths, lime, and dust!' He was probably even more astonished by the violence of Carlyle's reception.

'My darling,' wrote Jane to Kate Sterling, 'I could not leave home just now without the chance of finding Mr. C. in the prison on my return for having killed an Irish bricklayer because he had fallen through the ceiling!! Such incidents happen always *once* and sometimes *twice* in the day at present and it takes all my strength of mind to keep things from murder and utter insanity.' 'Pray', she begs, 'that the next man who falls in mayn't fall on my head and break my neck—one fell yesterday within a yard of the place I was standing on—it would be laughable if it didn't make so much mess. . . .' It was laughable, if, like Jane, you could make a joke of it. 'Had he dislocated my neck, as might so easily have happened,' she wrote to her brother-in-law, 'one of us would have been provided with a "silent apartment" enough, without further botheration.'

Apart from these unexpected and mutually alarming encounters, the Carlyles hardly set eyes on the men, who carried on their work out of sight (but not sound) of the rest of the house. Only Irish Fanny, who, it may be remembered, came out strong in the previous upheaval, enjoyed herself. Perhaps she was called upon to mop up one of her countrymen after a particularly violent tumble, and struck up a friendship; or perhaps the proximity of so many Irish went to her head. Somehow or other she fell from grace, and 'some time after,' said Carlyle, 'ran away into matrimony of a kind' with one of the Irish labourers. 'Run or walk away she did,' he continues, 'in the course of these dismal tumults, she too having gradually forgotten old things, and was never more heard of here.'

Soon after the fifth workman had fallen through the ceiling it was decided to accept Lady Ashburton's offer to stay at Addiscombe— 'beautifullest cottage in the world; the noble owners glad we would occupy a room or two of it in their absence. I liked it much,' said Carlyle, 'and kept busy reading, writing, riding.' But Jane, without these resources, grew restless. She did not like leaving Cheyne Row to the tender mercies of the Irish. And she had to find a new maid. She had hoped, she said to 'puddle on' for the present, turning a blind eye on Fanny's misdemeanours 'rather than front the horrors of change and a strange face in the house'. But evidently a crisis arose just before the Carlyles left for Addiscombe. After a week or two, 'I am again at Cheyne Row', she wrote to Kate Sterling, ' "superintending the works" and remoddling my household of *one woman*—Mr. C. *exploded* Fanny some fortnight ago—and I was vexed with him at the time . . . but now that the creature is fairly gone—even tho' I am in a state of interregnum I am glad. I have the old cook who was with me last year till I am suited— and I am going after a character tomorrow.' She was expected to rejoin her husband; but 'I shall be detained here,' she said, 'in the midst of disorder and noise and dirt for some days yet.' The attic stairs were being built and the house was 'about as uninhabitable as it was this time last year'. 'At Addiscombe', she adds, 'it is all so still and so lovely and Lady A.'s housemaid is so perfect in her doings—but there I do not feel *free*. . . .'

Carlyle remained at Addiscombe; and on 29 September wrote to John Forster: 'This is my third week of almost perfect Hermitism out here; such a life as I have rarely had experience of; for my wife is mostly at Chelsea, and for days together I literally do not speak one word! I think it is to end on Saturday.'

It did end, and a few days later, back at Cheyne Row, he 'got fairly in and *saw*' his new study. It was, he said, 'a spacious kind of place and very light; but sadly disappointing in one respect: it is of irregular shape in two of the walls, and in part two feet lower than I expected! . . . If it *be* soundproof,' he adds, '. . . certainly it will be a grand relief to me.' He was impatient to start work—'in any cell or safe inverted tub', as he put it; but the workmen showed no sign of finishing. On 28 November Carlyle was writing to his brother John, 'by Christmas, the undertaking is, they shall have finished, and be fairly gone'. Christmas! And the original estimate had been six weeks.

But what was more serious than its slow progress was the poor quality of the work. Carlyle had an eye for good workmanship, and he saw that the new study was not well built. He began to have his doubts about Chorley's confident prediction that the room would be insulated from noise, and as soon as he moved in he found that his doubts were confirmed. Moreover the stove wouldn't burn and the skylight let in a new assortment of sounds—river hooters, church bells and railway whistles.

'I fear my room is irremediably somewhat of a failure', he wrote, 'and that "quiet" is far off me yet!'

Jane was more dramatic. 'The silent room is the noisiest in the house,' she declared. 'Mr. C. is very much out of sorts.'

CHAPTER SEVEN

# Clothes

'BEING an only child', wrote Jane, 'I never wished to sew men's trowsers—no never!'

Carlyle was brought up in a household where it was taken for granted that the womenfolk made every shirt, nightshirt and pair of drawers worn by the father and brothers, and repaired their coats and trousers. When he married it was no doubt perplexing to him that his wife—so proficient in other ways—had never learned to sew. Her defence 'being an only child' became a family joke, and was often quoted.

'As for sewing,' she told Carlyle's sister Jean in 1849, 'you know that "being an only child I never wished to sew". Still, I have some inevitable work in that line, as even if I felt rich enough to have the "family needlework" done by others, I don't know where to find others to do it for money, without bothering me with their stupidity worse than if I did it myself.'

Being Jane, she quickly taught herself to sew in the early days of her marriage.★ At Craigenputtock she began virtuously making shirts. 'I am sitting here companionless,' she wrote in November 1828, 'having learnt my daily task of Spanish, and also finished a shirt—let me speak truth, a nightshirt—I was making for my husband.' And during the Craigenputtock days there are several pictures of Jane sewing. There in the depths of winter Carlyle writes of 'snow, black haze and deepest silence all round for miles', and within 'a blazing fire and a cap-making wife'.

But Jane was soon making other things as well as caps for herself. 'A well-fitting gown and a rather stylish bonnet' are reported in July 1833 to her friend Eliza Stodart; and when one thinks of the yards of skirt, the lined and boned bodice, and the big stiffened Gigot sleeves that were worn at that time, it must be conceded that —even if she did not follow the fashion slavishly—Jane had learnt to sew. The following November she made a pelerine.

'It is cut,' she told Eliza, 'out of some old lavender popelin which you must have seen officiating as a gown, not on one, but several members of our family, something like twenty years ago. . . . I realised out of it in the beginning of summer a singularly elegant bonnet; and the residue is now combining itself into a pelerine, which, lined with waddings and part of the old (villanously bad) crimson persian of the old cloak, will in the gracefullest manner protect my shoulders thro' the approaching inclemencies of the season.'

She 'never wished' to sew; but even in lonely Craigenputtock she wished to be elegant.

'O my dear cousin,' she exclaimed to Eliza, 'what a fine thing is a natural taste, especially for the wife of an Author, at a time when the booksellers' trade is so low!'

This natural taste for clothes never left her. Towards the end of her life we find her making 'a little jacket for home wear' out of a black silk scarf. 'The dressmakers who can fit one,' she told Mrs.

---

★'Husbands, I was shocked to find, wore their stockings into holes! and were always losing buttons! and *I* was expected to "look to all that".'

Russell, 'won't condescend to make anything but with their own materials. So I fell to cutting out that jacket last Monday, and only finished it today (Friday)! and was so much excited over the unusual nature of the enterprise (for I detest sewing, and don't sew for weeks together), that I could not leave off till the jacket was out of my hands.'

She was as proud of this jacket as she had been, thirty years before, of her home-made pelerine, and she offered the pattern to Mary Russell.

'But Lord preserve me,' she concludes, 'what a bother; better to have bought one ready-made at the dearest rate. I won't take a needle in my hands, except to sew on Mr. C.'s buttons, for the next six months.' Mr. C., when travelling, sewed on his own buttons; and carried a small supply in his writing case, together with needles, pins and two twists of thread.

To compensate for her dislike of sewing, Jane furnished herself with handsome appurtenances. Her silver sewing-case, designed to hang from her belt, was pretty as well as practical, and contained scissors, crochet-hook, bodkin, pencil—and a thimble on which were inscribed the words, 'Ah, me!' Her rosewood workbox had a tray which lifted out, divided into compartments holding small, flower-painted boxes containing tapes, buttons and hooks; there was a red silk cushion for pins and needles and a tiny mother-of-pearl reel containing an emery pad. The lower shelf held silks and cottons; and it may be noted that Carlyle could think of no better simile to describe the Admiralty cutter in which he sailed to Ostend —'clean as a lady's workbox'.

In spite of her protestations to the contrary, Jane enjoyed adventurous needlework. She would sit on the floor, crosslegged like a tailor, 'stitching, stitching' at the seams of a carpet; she would spend hours making herself a bonnet—'black silk and ermine and little feathers!'—when her right arm was crippled with neuritis. But she grumbled incessantly—to her friends if not to her husband —about the jobs she was expected to do, making and repairing his clothes.

'After tea', she wrote in 1849, 'there were certain accursed

flannel shirts (oh, the alterations that have been made to them!) to
"piece".'

'I am pressed for time . . . my nerves are all in a flurry . . . and
Mr. C. has just brought me an impossible glove to mend', she wrote
irritably in 1857. Mr. C. always seemed to bring her things to mend
when she was planning to write letters. ' "Jane, these cloth boots of
mine are in eminent need of some repair", or "Jane, these cloth
trousers of mine must have a new hem at the bottom".'

And on New Year's Day, 1863, 'Mr. C. suddenly discovered that
his salvation here and hereafter depended on having, "immediately,
without a moment's delay", a beggarly pair of old cloth boots' (the
same pair?) 'that the street-sweeper would hardly have thanked him
for, "lined with flannel, and new bound, and repaired generally".'
To do Mr. C. justice, he was suggesting that the job be given to one
of the servants, but Jane chose to flout the suggestion—'neither my
one woman, nor my half one, having any more capability of repairing these boots than of repairing the Great Eastern'—and do the
work herself. 'There was no help for me but to sit down on the
New Year's morning, with a great ugly beast of a man's boot in
my lap, and scheme, and stitch, and worry over it till night; and
next morning begin on the other!'

After they came to Chelsea, Jane must have made up her mind
that she was not going to go on making Carlyle's underclothes.
His youngest sister, Jenny, was the best seamstress of the family;
and in 1842 Carlyle sent this sister, now married and living in
Manchester, an order for summer shirts; as soon as she wrote that
they were finished he told her:

'I do not want them sent off yet till there are some more things
to go with them. I am in no want of them yet . . .' They could
wait, in fact, till the winter's barrel of oatmeal was sent from Scotsbrig to Chelsea. And meanwhile—

'Meanwhile I want you to make me some flannel things too—
three flannel shirts especially. . . . I have taken the measure today,
and now send you the dimensions, together with a measuring strap
which I bought some weeks ago (at one penny) for the purpose.'

'*You are to be careful to scour the flannel first*', he warns her, having evidently suffered from shirts shrunk in the wash. 'After which process the dimensions are these. *Width* (when the shirt is laid on its back) $22\frac{1}{2}$ inches, *extent from wrist button to wrist button* 61 inches, *length* in the back 35 inches, *length* in the front $25\frac{1}{2}$ inches. Do you understand all that?'

After assuring her that she has 'only to measure fair with the line and all will be right', he goes on, 'If you could make me two pairs of flannel drawers, I should like very well too. But that I am afraid', he adds—thinking perhaps of Jane—'will be too hard for you.'

It was not too hard. Jenny obliged, and at the end of October the barrel of meal and the box of garments arrived 'all safe' at Cheyne Row. Carlyle was delighted.

'I have to apprise you', he wrote to his sister, 'that *all fits* with perfect correctness. I have had a pair of drawers on, and a flannel shirt, I have one of the cambric shirts on me at present: everything is as right as if it had been made under my own eye.'

Jane was delighted too. The muslin shirts were 'excellently sewed'. 'She is the judge,' said her husband. The drawers, he told his sister, 'are the best fit of the article I have had for several years back'. Jenny had evidently made him not two but three pairs, two of the same flannel as the shirts, which he feared might prove '*too cool* for the depth of winter'; on the other hand, the third pair would be really warm, being made of 'right shaggy flannel'.

'My good Mother', he continues, 'sent a fine wool plaid too and a dozen pair of socks, few mortals are better off for woollen this winter!'

Carlyle felt the cold, and was careful to wrap up as thoroughly against the Chelsea winter as he ever did against the snows of Scotland.

'I have got me a *cloak* (of brown cloth, with fur neck)', he wrote in December 1834; 'a most comfortable article, in which I walk, in sharpest weather, as warm as a pie.' Jane and his mother searched the shops for snow-shoes for him. 'The best news', he told his mother in 1837, 'is that I have actually got, and do now wear, a pair of carpet-shoes exactly of the sort you were seeking for me! . . .

They are of black shag cloth, with three buttons, soft as wool; warm, light and comfortable beyond anything I have ever had on of that kind. They cost but some five-and-sixpence a pair out of the shops; mine were nine shillings, being made to order, and of a much larger size, the generality being for women only.' He urges his mother to get a pair—'and wear them within doors and without in winter time'.

In cold weather he also wore what he called 'wristikins', which prevented the wind from blowing up the sleeves of his overcoat. He did not like the pair Jane bought him: 'they are too slight, too *thin*, and do not fill up the cuff of the coat, which is rather wide with me'.

Jane's embargo on the manufacture of male garments included a refusal to knit. 'I dare say', Carlyle wrote hopefully to his sister Jenny, 'I dare say you can knit wristikins. It has struck me in these cold days I might as well apply to you to have a pair.' He still has the pair, he tells her, 'which either you, or I think Jean, knit for me at Hoddam Hill when you were little bairns many years ago. They have beautiful stripes of *red* yet, as fresh as ever.' What he wants, he continues, is something thick—'at least *double* the common thickness of those in the shops. If you had fine, *boozy* yarn and took it *two-ply* it will make a pretty article.' He would like if possible a deep red stripe, he adds, on a brown ground; and the breadth should be at least 3 inches.

The author of *Sartor Resartus* was fussy about his clothes. He was also conservative. Years after he had settled in London he was still having his suits made by the Ecclefechan tailor, who, in August 1843, was making him 'two pairs of trousers, two winter waistcoats, and much else in progress'. He was pleased with the trousers, except for their Dumfries buttons, which, he told Jane, 'I have duly execrated and flung aside.' Nothing good, it seemed, could come out of Dumfries; and buttons were of great importance. Henceforward they were ordered from London.

'Here are your bits of buttons, Dearest', Jane wrote, but went on to assure him that 'metal princes' feathers' or mother-o'-pearl, which he had asked for, would not do. 'Mother-o'-pearl! The bare idea,' said Jane, 'is enough to make one scream!' and she sent him something less fanciful, 'which, I think, will suit the taste of a philosopher better'.

She could not resist a dig at his loyalty to Ecclefechan products. 'When I said to Helen I must go to get some buttons for you, she tossed her head with an air of triumph and remarked, "Well, it's a mercy there is *one* thing which the Master fancies is to be got in *London* better than in the *Country!*"—a small mercy for which let us be duly grateful.'

Seven years later Carlyle wrote again from Scotsbrig asking for buttons.

' "If the buttons be here on Wednesday they will be in abundant time" ', quoted Jane sarcastically. 'I should think they would! and "don't you wish you may get them?" Why, how on earth could I have them there on Wednesday, unless, indeed, I had immediately last night, after reading your letter and swallowing my tea, dashed off in an omnibus to Regent Street, by dark; and then, having bought perhaps yellow buttons for drab ones, posted them before my return to Chelsea?'

Carlyle was no dandy, but he dressed with care and was particular that his neckwear should always be spotless. To the end of his life he wore the high old-fashioned satin stock and starched wing-collar of his youth—a fashion that derived from Brummell. In the early London days he made some attempt—encouraged by Jane—to dress like a Londoner. 'I have a new hat', he told his mother in 1834; 'and on Friday morning am to have a new frock-coat (of very dark "rifle green"): really a most smart man!' And a sketch of him by Maclise shows him in this tightly-fitting frock-coat, and holding a top hat, a form of head-gear not generally associated with Carlyle.

But the top hat was soon relegated to its box. In June 1836 he wrote triumphantly to his brother, 'I have got my white hat! A most noble broadbrim; price 6/6: of great comfort to me; and this not by the brim alone, I find, but also by the size, which lets in the air about me, and prevents the intrusion of headache: I find my last three or four hats have been far too little.'

At the sight of Carlyle in his white hat, Jane was horrified:

C.A.H.–H

shrieked, he said, and 'almost literally' wept. But he refused to give up his noble broad-brim, and in the end Jane was obliged to give in. 'She now says I do very well in it.' 'Cockneydom happily does not mind me at all', he added, 'tho' probably there is not such another beaver within the four ports of London.'

Beaver, felt or straw, from now on Carlyle's hats were invariably vast, and he wore them tilted over his eyes—'against headache'. His head, as well as his hat, was large, and he had thick, long hair. There is no doubt that his wide-brimmed hats suited him—and they *were* wide. 'The measure of my Hat, outside,' he wrote, 'is just two feet and one half inch, no more and no less.'

Jane gave way over his hats, but she still hoped to convert him to London tailoring. It cannot have been easy.

'My Husband,' she said, 'would almost as soon have an affair with a mad dog as with a Cockney shopman!' . . . 'He dislikes nothing in the world so much as going into a shop to buy anything, even his own trowsers and coats; so that, to the consternation of cockney tailors, I am obliged to go about them.' But Carlyle's faith in her judgement was shaken, she told Mrs. Russell, when she chose him a sky-blue coat 'with glorious *yellow* buttons, which made him an ornament to society in every direction'. 'Since then,' she continued, 'he has bought his own clothes very nicely; for it was not the want of judgement which hindered him so much as the want of will.'

But this statement proved optimistic. Carlyle, though he took an interest in what he wore, relied on Jane—particularly when he was immersed in a book—to keep him up to the mark. She gave up trying to make him smart: 'Carlyle's costume was always peculiar', wrote J. A. Froude: 'so peculiar thanks to his Ecclefechan tailor, that it was past being anxious about.' But she kept him tidy. 'I perceive', he wrote to her in 1857, 'you will have to set earnestly about getting me some wearing apparel when you come home. I have fallen quite shameful. I shall be naked altogether if you don't mind. Think of riding most of the summer with the aristocracy of the country . . . in a duffle jacket which literally was part of an old dressing-gown a year gone.'

Dressing-gowns were important to the Carlyles. They wore them for breakfast. 'By the time the table has been cleared . . . and oneself emerged out of dressing-gown into fit-to-be-seen-in gown eleven has probably struck', Jane wrote in 1842. 'To think there are women—Mrs. Carlyle for example—who spend £3. 14s. 6d. on one dressing-gown!' she noted in mock horror in her 'Budget of a *Femme Incomprise*'. The extravagance was justified: during her spells of illness and convalescence she spent whole days in a dressing-gown, only moving between her bedroom and the drawing-room, which were on the same floor.

In the autumn of 1837 she was suffering from a bad cough. Carlyle's mother tried in vain to buy her a warm dressing-gown, and was obliged to send her an umbrella instead. ('If I am not strong enough this winter to go out in the rain I will make a slight drizzle with the shower-bath and stand under it with my fine new umbrella', wrote Jane.) Her health improved, and a month later Carlyle reported that she had 'got a warm red tartan dressing-gown for the room, fur-tippet for the street'.

Dressing-gowns could be becoming as well as warm. After her street accident in 1863, when she lay for days and nights in agonizing pain, Carlyle remembered the night 'when her bedroom door (double door) suddenly opened upon me into the drawing-room, and she came limping and stooping on her staff, so gracefully and with such childlike joy and triumph, to irradiate my solitude. . . . She was in her Indian dressing-gown, absolutely beautiful.' Jeannie Welsh, too, could win admiration *en déshabille*. Keeping house for Carlyle while Jane was at Troston in 1842, she came down in the morning ' "in a kind of shawl *dressing gown, almost with the air of a little wife* to make coffee to me" '. The italics are Jane's, and she adds 'if there were a spark of jealousy in my disposition I would have taken out my seat in the next Bury coach, immediately upon reading that sentence! and returned in all haste to put a check to such dangerous illusions'.

Carlyle himself, in Robert Tait's painting, 'A Chelsea Interior', is wearing a very handsome dressing-gown of heavy striped silk. But in the early days at Cheyne Row he relied upon his mother's homespun wool to provide the garment in which he spent so many hours. He liked to wander about the garden, he told his mother in 1834, 'in dressing-gown and straw hat . . . and take my pipe in peace'. He hoped that she was making him a new one.

'For winter I left her the task of spinning me a plaid dressing gown', he told his brother; but the summer went by and no parcel arrived at Cheyne Row. Carlyle grew impatient. 'If I bring you a good *new Book* in my hand,' he wrote to his mother in September, 'will you not have that *new plaid dressing gown* ready for me!'

It was probably this garment which, according to his own account, he was wearing when, on 31 March 1839, the Count d'Orsay swept down Cheyne Row in his chariot 'that struck all Chelsea into mute astonishment with its splendour'.

The Phoebus Apollo of Dandyism, 'resplendent,' said Jane, 'as a diamond-beetle', descended from his sky-blue and silver coach and was shown upstairs to Jane's 'best room', lately embellished with a framed Dürer print and Mrs. Leigh Hunt's bust of Shelley. Glancing at the latter, d'Orsay remarked, 'Ah! It is one of those faces who weesh to swallow their chin!' and seated himself—careful for his coat-tails—opposite his host. Jane, sitting a little way off, observed the scene with amusement. 'A sight it was to make one think the millennium actually at hand,' she told her mother, 'when the lion and the lamb, and all incompatible things should consort together.'

D'Orsay wore a 'skye-blue satin cravat . . . with white French gloves, light drab overcoat lined with velvet of the same colour, invisible inexpressibles, skin-coloured and fitting like a glove'. His ornaments, she remembered later, consisted of 'two glorious breast-pins attached by a chain, and length enough of gold watch-guard to have hanged himself in'.

'Jane laughed for two days,' said Carlyle, 'at the contrast of my plaid dressing gown, bilious iron countenance, and this Paphian apparition.'

A few weeks later the Carlyles dined at 'd'Orsaydom or Blessing-tondom'. 'D'Orsay,' said Carlyle, 'is decidedly clever and no bad fellow; he drew a fine portrait of me in the drawing-room, really very like.' In this drawing the Chelsea philosopher is seen in profile, wearing a high stock and starched collar up to his ears; his dress coat with its velvet collar evidently the product of a London tailor. The contrast, at this meeting, between the Man of Genius and the Man of Fashion, cannot have been so marked.

'Poor d'Orsay!' wrote Jane six years later. 'He was born to have been something better than the king of dandies.' On 13 April 1845 he paid his second visit to Cheyne Row.

'I had not seen him,' she said, 'for four or five years. Last time he was gay in his colours as a humming-bird. . . . Today, in compliment to his five more years, he was all in black and brown— a black satin cravat, a brown velvet waistcoat, a brown coat, some shades darker than the waistcoat, lined with velvet of its own shade, and almost black trousers, *one* breast-pin, a large pear-shaped pearl set into a little cup of diamonds, and only one fold of gold chain round his neck, tucked together right on the centre of his spacious breast with one magnificent turquoise. Well! that man understood his trade; but if it be but that of a dandy, nobody can deny that he is a perfect master of it, and dresses himself with consummate skill.'

Another celebrated visitor had less confidence in his appearance.

In February 1843, Macready, the actor, called with his wife. The Carlyles had seen many of his performances.

'Macready, the Manager of Covent Garden, a classical man wishing to banish the wild beasts and gather "Intellect" around him, has most unexpectedly sent me a Free admission for the season', Carlyle wrote in 1837, 'and I go some once a week hither to see some Shakespeare notability or the like: really not without some enjoyment: last night we had *Macbeth*, deeply impressive in some parts, totally distracted in others. . . . A wild rough sincerity is in (Macready), really a kind of genius; I hope to know the man personally yet.' This hope was realized: Macready attended Carlyle's lectures, and the admiration became mutual. But the Macreadys' visit in 1843 appears to have been their first.

'Poor dear William!' Jane wrote to Helen Welsh, 'I never thought him more interesting. To see a man, who is exhibiting himself every night on a stage, blushing like a young girl in a private room is a beautiful phenomenon for me. His wife whispered into my ear, as we sat on the sofa together, "Do you know poor William is in a perfect agony today at having been brought here in that great-coat? It is a stage great-coat, but was only worn by him twice; the piece it was made for did not succeed, but it was such an expensive coat, I would not let him give it away; and doesn't he look well in it?" '

He did look well, Jane added. 'I wish Jeannie had seen him in the coat—magnificent fur neck and sleeves, and such frogs on the front.' So there was no need for the great man to look 'so heartily ashamed of himself'. In his diary the only comment he makes upon this visit is 'I was amused'; so evidently in the Carlyles' company he forgot his discomfiture.

It will be seen that Jane possessed a keen eye for dress. Even as a child she took a lively interest in what she wore. Carlyle in his *Reminiscences* paints a charming picture of the infant Jane, 'tripping nimbly and daintily along, her little satchel in hand, dressed by her mother (who had a great talent that way) in tasteful simplicity; neat bit of pelisse (light blue sometimes), fastened with black belt, dainty little cap, perhaps little beaverkin (with flap turned up), and I think one at least with a modest little plume in it.' And she herself was able, forty-two years later, to describe the ball-dress she wore at the age of 9.

'I can tell you every item in it', she wrote: 'a white Indian muslin frock open behind, and trimmed with *twelve* rows of satin ribbon; a broad white satin sash reaching to my heels; little white kid shoes, and embroidered silk stockings—which last are in a box upstairs along with the cap I was christened in!'

She always, by her own ingenuity, managed to dress with elegance. She had a pretty figure, and held herself very upright; and she was invariably neat, favouring velvet bands at her neck and wrists, and little collars of lawn or lace. She was not always conventional in dress. At a time when no lady would venture out of doors without first putting on bonnet, shawl and gloves, Jane would run down the street to see off a guest from the Cadogan Pier without bothering to do more than snatch up something to put on her head. Henry Taylor complimented her: she was 'the first woman he had ever found in this world who could go out of her house without at least a quarter of an hour's preparation'.

'Alas, that England should expect of one to wear caps "at a certain age", for all that one's hair don't turn grey!'

Jane liked to wear her smooth black hair uncovered, and many of her portraits show her without the conventional cap. Sitting for her painting by Gambardella, in March 1843, she flung a black lace scarf over her head, which suited her gipsy looks; but she had not the courage to appear in this head-dress at a party a few days later. 'Spiteful people would say "Mrs. Carlyle being desperate of enacting the *girlish* any longer with advantage, is now for doing the *nun-like*" ' —so she twisted a wreath of flowers round her 'small knob of hair— with what effect those who found themselves *behind* me only know'.

In 1862, being photographed unexpectedly 'by the best photographer in London' (W. Jeffrey in Great Russell Street), she was obliged to borrow a cap from the photographer's aunt, who 'offered me a white lace thing, so like one of my *own* loose caps, that I put it on without reluctance; and the same helpful woman, seeing the black lace I wear round my neck lying on the table, snatched it up and suggested I should be done also in that headdress'. Fortunately she was wearing a well-cut dress, she said, which gave her a good figure.

The well-cut dress had a tightly fitting bodice, frogged across the chest, with bishop sleeves. The very full skirt was organ-pleated into the waist at the back, with looser gathers in front, where it opened over a stiff brocaded silk petticoat. This was her last winter's gown, made by a London dressmaker, Madame Élise. It was fashionable at all points but one: it had no crinoline. Jane would not wear one.

When she first came to London in the 1830's, skirts were growing fuller and were padded out at the back. 'The diameter of the fashionable ladies', she wrote to her mother in 1834, 'at present is about three yards; their bustles (false bottoms) are the size of an ordinary sheep's fleece. The very servant-girls wear bustles: Eliza Miles told me a maid of theirs went out one Sunday with three kitchen dusters pinned on as a substitute.'

In the 1840's skirts were wider still, flounced, and reinforced by petticoats. Then in 1855 the Empress Eugénie visited England; her influence on fashion was strong. In 1856 the crinoline, a framework made of whalebone and worn over the petticoats, arrived. Crinolines grew larger and larger. Special arm-chairs were designed to allow for the overflow of billowing skirts, and in *Punch* John Leech made jokes about the many predicaments in which ladies were landed by these monstrous contraptions. In 1858 a ladies' magazine advised an inquirer 'not to attempt the climbing of stiles in a crinoline, for the task is impossible; and if she suffers much from the comments of vulgar little boys it would be better, in a high wind, to remain indoors'.

Even servants wore crinolines, which must have been most awkward when they were at work.

'When the rooms are done', Jane wrote to her husband in 1864, 'pray charge the maids not to rub on the clean paper with their abominably large crinolines.'

But she herself never wore one. Nor would she tight-lace. In the same year, 1864, she went to Madame Élise to have a new dress fitted.

'I was before the time of day for the fashionable ladies, so Élise was disengaged and came to the fitting-room herself, to superintend the process. . . . And she would not let me have the thing done *anyhow*, as I wanted, saying to her French dressmaker: "Because Madame *will not* wear a crinoline and will not be tied up, *that* is no reason why she should have no waist and no style!" '

Madame Élise was a fashionable and highly successful dressmaker, who thought nothing of charging £300 for a dress if she considered that the customer could afford it. But she liked and admired Mrs. Carlyle and charged her accordingly.

In 1862 Jane ordered a new evening gown for a visit to the Ashburtons.

'Élise got me up in a rose coloured petticoat, with black tunic (good god!) which made me the envy of surrounding women. "Quite a *costume*!" said one. "May I ask, Mrs. Carlyle, what Madame Élise charged you for that dress?" said another (Emily

Baring). "No—you may *not*!" I answered, "I can only tell you, it was not more than I could easily pay!" '

This arresting 'costume' was described in detail to Mrs. Russell.

'But the rose-coloured petticoat—oh, my Dear! I must tell you about the appearance of *that*! I put it on the second day, and the black silk tunic trimmed with half-a-yard-wide lace (imitation), with long falling sleeves lined with rose-colour; and a great bunch of rose-coloured ribbon on my breast, and smaller bows at the wrists of my white under-sleeves.'

Unfortunately, the rose-coloured petticoat dipped in front, and nearly tripped her up when she made her embarrassed entrance—late—in to dinner. Later in the evening, guests and family attended prayers. 'Eight-and-thirty servants were seated along two sides of the room; the men all in a line, and the women all in a line; and with those thirty-eight pairs of eyes on me (six pairs of them belonging to Ladies' maids!!) I had to sail up, in all that rose-colour, to the top of the room. . . . And the same in going out; I had to walk the length of the room, like to trip myself at every step, with the petticoat and the embarrassment! before that frightful line of servants budged.'

But this dress, with its rose-coloured petticoat and bunches of ribbons, became a favourite garment: two years later she was wearing the black silk tunic '*every* day and *all* day'; it had fairly gone to tatters, she told Mrs. Russell—'and no shame to it'.

But after her serious illness in 1864 she began to shed her bright plumage.

'White lace and red roses don't become a woman who has been looking both death and insanity in the face for a year', she wrote, after a visit to Élise, 'to get the velvet bonnet she made me last year stripped of its finery.'

Two months later, in her sober bonnet, she went to take a 'dinner-tea' with Madame Élise, who must have been a remarkable woman. She had a magnificent house at Acton—'an old manor house, with endless passages; and at every turn of the passage there is a bust—Lord Byron, Sir Walter Scott, Pope, Milton, Locke. . . .'

'There is an immense garden round the house, with greenhouses

and a great green field beyond the garden, with sheep in it! . . .
A middle-aged ladylike governess took charge of the three children:
perfect little beauties! and the nurse and other maids had the air of a
"great family" about them. They all treated "Madame" as if she
had been a princess! A triumph of genius!'

Madame, with her own carriage and her fine estate, appears to
have been a rare specimen in her day—a successful business woman,
who had turned her natural gift for *haute couture* to good effect.

'The only drawback to my satisfaction', wrote Jane after this
visit, 'was a dread of catching cold.' In this period of her life that
dread was with her always. In cold weather she wore layer upon
layer of flannel petticoats, and ordered herself 'two new ones made
out of a pair of Scotch blankets'. To her delight, Lady Sandwich
sent her a sealskin pelisse—'a luxury I had long sighed for, but
costing twenty guineas, it had seemed hopeless!' Out driving, or
lying on her sofa, she rolled herself in 'a coverlet of racoon skins';
and the Greek merchant Dilberoglue, who gave her her dog Nero,
sent her a soft grey Indian shawl.

The Cheyne Row house was, as we have seen, draughty,
particularly when the wind blew from the east. 'To see the fires
I keep up in the drawing-room and my bedroom!' Jane wrote in the
winter of 1862. But even with big fires there were draughts: in
houses great and small women of all classes huddled into shawls to
keep their shoulders and backs warm.

One February night in 1863 a very handsome long woollen shawl
arrived for Jane by the Parcel Delivery Company. It was sent by an
anonymous admirer of Carlyle, who wrote, 'My obligations to your
husband are many and unnameably great, and I just wish to
acknowledge them.'

'We are both equally gratified, and thank you heartily', Jane
wrote. 'When the shawl came . . . Mr. C. himself wrapped it
about me, and walked round me admiring it. And what do you
think he said? He said: "I am very glad of that for you, my dear.
I think it is the only bit of real good my celebrity ever brought
you!" '

Fashion demanded that Victorian ladies, who presented such a

modest appearance by day, should bare their white shoulders and
bosoms by night. Just before Jane's forty-ninth birthday the Carlyles
were invited to a ball at Bath House. Jane, always reluctant to accept
Lady Ashburton's invitations, was for declining; but 'Mr. C. was
"quite determined for once in his life" to see an aristocratic Ball
and "if I chose to be so peevish and ungracious as to stay away there
was no help for me". I pleaded the want of a dress—he "would pay
for any dress I chose to get".'

Jane had not, as yet, discovered the invaluable Élise; she was
obliged to decide for herself what to wear. 'So I got a white silk
dress . . . made high and long-sleeved.' But it would not do.
Everyone, said Carlyle, would be *décolletée*. All Jane's Puritan blood
rose up in horror at the idea of 'stripping' herself—'of being bare
at my age after being muffled up for so many years'. There was a
scene. 'True propriety,' declared Carlyle, consisted in conforming
to other people's fashions—'and that Eve he supposed had as much
sense of decency as I had and *she* wore no clothes at all!!!'

So the dress was sent back, to be cut down to what Jane called
'the due pitch of indecency'. 'I could have gone into fits of crying',
she wrote, 'when I began to put it on—but I looked so astonishingly
well in it by *candle-light*, and when I got into the fine rooms amongst
the universally *bare* people I felt so much in *keeping*, that I forgot my
neck and arms almost immediately.' Afterwards she admitted she
was glad that she had gone—'not for any pleasure I had at the time,
being past dancing, and knowing but few people—but it is an
additional idea for life, to have seen such a party—all the Duchesses
one ever heard tell of blazing in diamonds, all the young beauties of
the season, all the distinguished statesmen . . . and all the rooms
hung with artificial roses looked like an Arabian Nights entertainment'. 'Lady Ashburton receiving all these people with her grand-
Lady airs was also a sight worth seeing,' added Jane drily.

The ball left a lasting impression—a much stronger one than did
her meeting with Charlotte Brontë, a day or two later. 'Extremely
unimpressive to *look at*', was Jane's only comment, and Miss Brontë's
dress went unnoticed.

Both Carlyles took a lively interest in clothes, and described any costume that took their fancy, either for its own sake or on account of its wearer. Men's fashions, in the 1840's, were varied and sometimes original.

While Jane was away, in the summer of 1842, Carlyle accepted an invitation to join Stephen Spring Rice, the Commissioner of Customs, on a short trip to Ostend in an Admiralty yacht. He wrote a graphic account of his adventures, calling it 'The Shortest Tour on Record', and in it he described the 'astonishing' garments worn by Spring Rice and his brother Charles when they arrived in Belgium. While the captain of the yacht, and Carlyle himself, wore 'rational English costume', the Spring Rice brothers drew curious stares from the inhabitants of Bruges. 'The Home Commissioner,' he said, 'in a pair of coarsest blue shag trousers, with a horrible blue shag spencer without a waistcoat, and a scanty blue cap on his head, had a truly *flibustier* air. The good Charles had a low-crowned, broad-brimmed glazed hat, ugliest of hats, and one of those amazing sack coats which the English dandies have taken to wear, the make of which is the simplest. One straight sack to hold your body, two smaller sacks on top for the arms, and by way of collar a hem. The earliest tailor on earth would make his coat even so; and the Bond Street snip has returned to that as elegance.'

When he was back in Chelsea, with Jeannie Welsh (Babbie), to minister to his comfort, Jane wrote from Troston in Suffolk describing a visit to the grandees of the district, Mr. and Lady Agnes Byng (who had been born a Paget).

' "The Pagets" seem to be extremely like other mortals,' she said, 'neither better nor bonnier nor wiser. To do them justice, however, they might, as we found them, have been sitting for a picture of high life doing the amiable and the rural in the country. They had placed a table under the shadow of a beech-tree; and at this sat Mr. Byng studying the "Examiner"; Lady Agnes reading— "oh, nothing at all, only some nonsense that Lord Londonderry has been printing; I cannot think what has tempted him". . . . I may mention for your consolation,' she told Carlyle, 'that Mr. Byng was dressed from head to foot in unbleached linen; while Babbie may take a slight satisfaction to her curiosity *de femme* from knowing how a Paget attires herself of a morning, to sit under a beech tree—a white-flowered muslin pelisse, over pale blue satin; a black lace scarf fastened against her heart with a little gold horse-shoe; her white neck tolerably revealed, and set off with a brooch of diamonds; immense gold bracelets, an immense gold chain; a little white silk bonnet with a profusion of blond and flowers; thus had she prepared herself for being rural!'

A fortnight later her hosts suggested a second call upon Lady Agnes.

'Lady Agnes! and I in my wearing gown!—absolutely *fringed* round the skirt with *rags* as no woman unless lost to all sense of shame would like to present herself to a be-satined and be-diamonded Lady Agnes. I had to run and strip and re-clothe myself with the speed of a house on fire . . .' So speedy was she that she discovered afterwards that she had paid her respects to the aristocracy wearing odd stockings.

Nine years later, when her acquaintance with the nobility was wider, she continued to observe and describe with her own blend of *naïveté* and cynicism. Staying with the Stanleys at Alderley Park in September 1851, she was shown Lady Blanche's trousseau, and commented, 'I saw a *trousseau* for the first time in my life; about as wonderful a piece of nonsense as the Exhibition of All Nations. Good Heavens! how is any one woman to use up all those gowns and cloaks and fine clothes of every denomination? And the profusion of coronets! every stocking, every pocket handkerchief, everything had a coronet on it!'

'Gainsborough should have been alive to paint her', wrote Anne Thackeray, remembering her first impressions of Jane when she and her sister, as little girls, visited the Cheyne Row house. 'Slim, bright, dark-eyed, upright . . . she looked like one of the grand ladies our father used sometimes to take us to call upon. She used to be handsomely dressed in velvet and point lace.'

It would seem that Jane, watching with detached curiosity and interest the grand ladies of her acquaintance, succeeded in acquiring something of their manner, allying it to her own natural dignity.

She wore little or no jewellery. Her wedding ring was a narrow hoop of gold; on the third and fourth fingers of her right hand she sometimes wore two small rings each containing a single stone; and there was a curious little gilt ring with a design of dolphins which she wore constantly. She was wearing it when she died. In 1862 she gave two brooches to Mary Russell: 'the brooches can be worn as clasps, down the front of the dress, also; and look very well on a dress of any colour'. She accepted in exchange an old pebble brooch in the shape of a thistle, which had once been her own—'my Mother was with me when I was allowed to choose it! and my Father paid for it!'—and which she took back out of sentiment. She also possessed a seed-pearl brooch made like a Maltese cross; and on her forty-sixth birthday Carlyle gave her a cameo brooch, which she received without enthusiasm: 'I cannot tell you how it is, but his gifts always distress me more than a scold from him would do,' she told Helen Welsh. Another pebble brooch, set in silver, she gave away to Miss Craik; and to Macready, playing Macbeth, she presented an old Scottish brooch that had belonged to Flora Macdonald.

A tiny gold basket containing mounted hair, 'a beautiful little thing as ever I beheld!' she considered 'too beautiful and too youthful for the individual intended to wear it'. She attached it to her bracelet, but wondered 'whether I ought not to have my nose pierced and suspend it from that.'

Though Jane possessed few jewels, she clearly did not hanker for more. She did not need them. Staying at The Grange, she watched, amused, the 'young married ladies . . . all vieing with each other who to be finest', and declared that 'the blaze of diamonds every day at dinner, quite took the shine out of the chandeliers'. But Jane, without a single diamond, could outshine them all. As Forster said of her, 'With some of the highest gifts of intellect, and the charm of a most varied knowledge of books and things, there was something "beyond, beyond".'

CHAPTER EIGHT

## *Creatures Great and Small*

CHRISTMAS in the 1840s was the occasion—as indeed it still is—for a great slaughtering of beasts and birds; and butchers' shops in Chelsea were filled with gruesome works of art, decorated, as Jane noted in horrified fascination, with holly, and 'very coquettish bows' of blue and red ribbon. 'A number of persons,' she said, were gazing at the arrangement of dead animals in one shop window, 'with a grave admiration beyond anything I ever saw testified towards any picture in the National Gallery! The butcher himself was standing beside it, receiving their silent enthusiasm with a look of Artist-pride struggling to keep within the bounds of Christian humility.'

'Last Christmas,' she remembered, 'another of our Chelsea butchers . . . regaled the public with the spectacle of a *living* prize-calf, on the breast of which (poor wretch) was branded—like writing on turf—"6d. per lb." And the public gathered about this unfortunate with the greedy looks of cannibals.'

Poor wretch indeed. Jane, at Craigenputtock, could walk through the farmyard and single out chickens and geese for killing; but London butchery with its grim showmanship shocked her. She had a tender heart for the sufferings of animals.

'Poor beast! I could have cried for him', she wrote of Carlyle's horse Fritz, who, in his old age, was being broken to run in harness. And after going to a pheasant shoot in 1860 she wrote, 'The firing made me perfectly sick. Think of the bodily and mental state of the surviving birds when the day's sport was ended. Decidedly, men can be very great brutes when they like.'

In spite of all that they suffered from the noises made by other people's animals and birds, the Carlyles were never without some form of 'dumb creature' at Cheyne Row. 'After I had been in London a short time', Jane wrote, 'my husband advised me—ironically of course—to put an advertisement in the window "House of Refuge for stray dogs and cats". The number of dogs and cats in distressed circumstances who imposed themselves on my country simplicity was in fact prodigious.'

Such lavish hospitality could not continue; but there was generally a cat, often kittens; there were canaries, and—for nearly eleven years—there was Mrs. Carlyle's dog, Nero.

There were also the uninvited creatures.

'Mr. C., in the midst of talking to me the other evening, suddenly stamped his foot on the hearth-rug and called out furiously "Get along, sir!" and he had not gone mad, had merely perceived a mouse at his feet!'

Regiments of mice, said Jane, had effected a settlement in every part of the house, and 'threaten to run up one's very petticoats while one is reading one's book'.

A new cat would have to be installed without delay. The dirty house next door (number 6, of course!) was probably responsible for the mice, which made their way into number 5 as soon as they knew there was no cat.

The last cat had been drowned, during Jane's absence, for 'un-exampled dishonesty'. The new cat, a young black female, to be known—for reasons which will appear later—as Columbine, arrived, and in due course the regiments of mice retreated.

The old house, with its panelled walls and thick uneven floors, its closets and presses with ill-fitting doors, provided comfortable shelter for innumerable unwanted creatures. Bugs, as we have seen, were at this time a prevalent menace in town houses. 'We have no bugs yet', Jane wrote proudly in 1835; '. . . and I do not know of one other house among all my acquaintance that so much can be said for.'

These unpleasant creatures, as we have already noticed, took possession of Helen's bed in the front kitchen, and the bed had to be removed before they could be eliminated. Another horrible discovery was made in 1849, this time in Jane's own 'red bed'. She was appalled. 'All my curtains,' she said, 'have been frantically torn down and sent to the dyers; not so much to have the colour renewed, as to have the bugs boiled to death.'

Careless maids and lack of fresh air while master and mistress were away brought about further invasions. In 1856, after their return from Scotland, 'My dear,' said Carlyle over the breakfast table—these announcements always seemed to be made over the breakfast table—'My dear, I have to inform you that my bed is full of bugs, or fleas, or some sort of animals that crawl over me all night.'

Jane received the news sceptically. 'Living in a universe of bugs outside, I had entirely ceased to fear them in my own house,' she said, 'having kept it for so many years perfectly clean from all such abominations.' 'But clearly,' she continued, 'the practical thing to be done was to go and examine his bed. . . . So, instead of getting into a controversy that had no basis, I proceeded to toss over his blankets and pillows, with a certain sense of injury! But on a sudden, I paused in my operations; I stooped to look at something the size of a pin-point; a cold shudder ran over me; as sure as I lived it was an infant bug! And, oh, heaven, that bug, little as it was, must have parents—grandfathers and grandmothers, perhaps!' She went on looking, she said, with 'frenzied minuteness' and her fears were

confirmed. A carpenter was fetched post-haste to take down the
bed. 'The next three days,' she said, 'I seemed to be in the thick of a
domestic Balaklava.' The maid, Ann, was 'indignant that the house
should be turned up after she had "settled it", and that "such a
fuss should be made about bugs, which are inevitable in London".
There was a scene. Ann declared "It was to be hoped I would get a
person to keep my house cleaner than she had done; as she meant
to leave that day month!" To which I answered "Very good," and
nothing more.'

Ann did not leave, however; and some six weeks later she figured
in a domestic drama caused by another species of pest.

'I have a servant', wrote Jane, 'whom during the five years she
has been with me, I had never seen in a hurry, or excited, or
deprived of her presence of mind. What then was my astonishment
when she rushed into the drawing-room last night, with her head
*tumbled off* (as at first it looked to me) and carrying it in her hands!!
and crying wildly, "Oh Ma'am! I must go to a Doctor (*scream*). My
ear, my ear! (*scream*). An animal has run into my ear!!" She was
holding down her head as low as her waist, her cap off, her hair
flying, and her hand pressed to her right ear. I sprang forward and
pulled her fingers from her ear which was full of blood. "*What
animal?*" I gasped. "Oh, I think it is a black beetle!!"—And the
screams went on, and she declared the beetle was "running up into
her brain". Her ignorance of anatomy was very unfortunate at the
moment! I called up Mr. Carlyle; for I had lost all presence of mind,
as well as herself. He took it coolly, as he takes most things.
"Syringe it,' he said; "syringing will bring out any amount of black
beetles." .

'There is an Apothecary at the bottom of our street; I threw
a table cover about her, and told her to run to him; and I begged
Mr. C. to go with her, as it was a dangerous thing for me to go out
in the night air. "Go with her?" he said, "What good could it do *my*
seeing the beetle taken out of her ear?"—But I had read in a newspaper, not long ago, of a man killed by some insect creeping into his
ear; and how did I know that the Apothecary was not an ass, and
might spoil her hearing for life, with probes and things,—if indeed

she did not die of it, or go raving mad, as I should do in her place, I thought?—I paced up and down the room for some ten minutes like a wild animal in its cage; then put on a cloak and bonnet and rushed after her, Mr. C. running after *me* to pull me back.'

When Jane arrived at the Apothecary's she found Ann covered in soap-suds. The man had acted quickly; and the beetle—'it actually was a black-beetle,' said Jane—had been removed, more or less intact. 'There might be a leg or so left,' said the Apothecary, offering to syringe the ear again in the morning. But Ann had had enough, and the ear was left to recover without further treatment. 'Meanwhile,' said Jane, 'I feel as if I had been pounded with a mortar, with the fright of the thing.'

Jane, clearing out kitchen cupboards in 1850, after the final departure of Helen, found that 'many an abomination came to light': and it was just such abominations, and crumbs of food lying unnoticed in dark corners, that brought the black-beetles, marching like prunes with legs, in close formation, through many a Victorian kitchen. They were accepted as inevitable; such masses were hard to destroy, and they disappeared as soon as it was light, into their hidden holes. Unlike mice, they were undeterred by the presence of a cat; and as, on the whole, they did no harm, beyond leaving an unpleasant smell, they were generally left to their own devices. Mice, on the other hand, were known to be dirty. They ran over the food in the cupboards and left droppings and tooth-marks in the butter and cheese, they climbed on to shelves and ate everything they could find; they fell into the milk and drowned, they dragged pieces of bread across the floor and left mouldering crumbs inside the wainscots.

There had to be a cat.

These cats were part of the household machinery; they ate what they could get, and lived where they worked, in the basement. For Jane a cat was not a pet, but a practical necessity; but Carlyle had a soft spot for cats, which continued into his old age.

'We have got a nice large fat cat here', his niece Mary Aitken wrote in 1874, to a child called Miss Sally Norton. 'Mr. Carlyle likes it so much. He takes the hearth brush every morning and smoothes down its fur; puss likes it exceedingly and stretches herself out when she sees him coming; she shuts her eyes and pretends to be asleep.'

During Helen's reign there was a high-spirited cat which Jane found altogether too lively. Any affection that it had was given to Helen, who declared, said Jane, 'It is the strangest cat, just *dottedly* fond of her!' 'In what manner it had expressed its *adoration*,' added Jane sarcastically, 'I could not discover.'

There were ups and downs in the friendship, however. For this was the cat which Helen 'all but killed with the besom' when it ran off with her red herring. But the cat survived, and we hear of her the following summer, playing in the garden with Dr. John Carlyle. She had several families which had to be disposed of; and in 1844 she took advantage of Carlyle's absence in Scotland to give birth to two kittens in his bed.

'We have drowned them,' said Jane, 'and now she . . . is coming about my feet mewing in a way that quite wrings my heart. Poor thing! I never saw her take on so badly before.'

It was probably this same unfortunate cat whose 'unexampled dishonesty' brought about her sad end, in the river. Who carried out this harsh sentence is not known. It may well have been Helen, who only a few months later attempted to make an end of herself in the same way.

The next cat was Columbine, the only one to have a name. 'The new cat,' said Jane, 'seems full of good dispositions'; but she only survived for three years. In 1852 a white cat of uncertain sex took up residence. It had a bad start, for an earthquake was in progress, the kitchen occupied by plumbers boiling lead, and the garden filled with scaffolding and other impedimenta.

Evidently frighted by the uproar and discomfort, it ran away. 'I suppose she couldn't stand the muddle,' said Jane philosophically, and considered an offer from Darwin of 'a cat with a bad heart'. But the white cat came back—only to disappear again a few months later—'for a whole day and night together'. 'He or she (whichever its worthy sex)', wrote Jane, 'having gone by the garden wall, returned by the front area. A clever cat, this one, evidently, but of an unsettled turn of mind.'

In September 1858—the white cat having either died or run away for good—Charlotte the young servant found a new invasion of mice and 'took the liberty' of installing a kitten. Jane, returning from Scotland, was pleased. 'An unexpected joy!' she wrote to Mary Russell, 'a jet-black kitten added to the household! playing with the dog as lovingly as your cat with your dog! This acquisition of my Charlotte's announced itself to me by leaping on to my back between my shoulders. A most agile kitten, and wonderfully confiding.'

But alas, this charming kitten grew, as kittens do, into a cat.

'*That cat*!!' wrote Jane in 1865—'I wish she were dead! but *I* can't shorten her days because—you see—my poor dear wee dog liked her! Well! there she is—and as long as she attends Mr. C. at his meals (she doesn't care a snuff of tobacco for him at other times) so long will Mr. C. continue to give her bits of meat, and driblets of milk, to the ruination of carpets and hearthrugs!'

'He has no idea', she concluded, 'what a selfish, immoral, improper beast she is.'

Jane had crossed swords with this cat five years before when the 'selfish, immoral, improper beast' had, as she put it, attempted a great crime. 'For several days', she wrote, 'there had been *that* in her eyes when raised to my canary, which filled my heart with alarm. I sent express for a carpenter, and had the cage attached to the drawing-room ceiling, with an elaborate apparatus of chain and pulley and weight. . . . And there it had swung for two days, to Mr. C.'s intense disgust, who regards this pet as "*the most inanely chimerical of all*"—the cat meanwhile spending all its spare time in gazing up at the bird with eyes aflame! But it was safe *now*, I thought! and went out for a walk. On my return Charlotte met me with "Oh! whatever *do* you think the cat has gone and done?" "Eaten my canary?"—"No, *far worse*!—pulled down the cage and the weight, and broke the chain and upset the little table and broken everything on it!"—"And not eaten the canary?"—"Oh, I suppose the dreadful crash she made frightened *herself*; for I met *her* running downstairs as I ran up—tho' the cage was on the floor, and the door open and the canary in such a way!" '

'That,' said Jane, 'is what one gets from breeding up a cat.'

It was not the first time that a cat had 'gazed with eyes aflame' at Jane's birds.

It may be remembered that when the Carlyles arrived at Cheyne Row in 1834 they brought with them a canary called Chico. As soon as they had settled down Jane found him a wife: and in the course of nature they produced, said Carlyle, 'two bright yellow young ones'. But in the summer of 1835 Jane wrote to Mrs. Aitken of 'a disaster befallen me since I commenced this letter—the cat has eaten one of my canaries! Not Chico, poor dear; but a young one which I hatched myself.'

She would have nothing more to do with the cat. 'I have sent the abominable monster out of my sight for ever—transferred her to Mrs. Hunt.' No doubt the Leigh Hunts had plenty of mice to distract the cat's attention from canaries.

But Chico came to a bad end. Carlyle makes no mention of the cat, but writes that the bright yellow young ones, 'as soon as they were fledged, got out into the trees of the garden, and vanished towards swift destruction; upon which, villain Chico finding his poor wife fallen so tattery and ugly, took to pecking a hole in her head, pecked it and killed her, by and by ending his own disreputable life'.

After the death of Chico there were no more birds for twenty years. But in 1856 Jane wrote to Carlyle from Scotland that she would be bringing home '—oh gracious! I picture your dismay!— whatever will you say or sing?—two live—ca-ca-naries!' These birds endeared themselves to her because they came from her parents' old home in Haddington. She took them with her on a round of visits, with 'a black silk bag to draw over the cage . . . trimmed with braid'. 'You may still hope,' she told Carlyle, 'that they shall get eaten by my aunt's cat, or my cousin's terrier, or at least, by the cat or Nero at home. But I hope better things. . . .'

After difficult journeys by train and boat—'the Birdcage was caught out of my arms by a stranger lady' when Jane was overcome by sea-sickness—she arrived home with the canaries at the end of

September. Fortunately, Carlyle accepted them calmly: 'truth to say, I rather expected he would wring their necks!'

'The canaries are the happiest creatures in the house', she wrote the following January.

Like Chico, they lived in the back dining-room.

'I have not been well enough to go down to breakfast for upwards of eight weeks,' wrote Jane, 'but the other morning, the doors being all open, I was thunderstruck to hear my young friends chirruping at the very top of their lungs! When Mr. C. came into my room soon after, I apologised for the disturbance, and spoke of removing the cage. "Oh let them alone there!" said he, "the little wretches have been all this time as *merry as maltsters*! But their incessant distracted chirling rather amuses me!"'

A year later, one of the birds took to falling off its perch, lying helplessly on its back till Jane picked it up and replaced it. 'What a blessing,' she said, 'to have somebody to always lift one up when one falls off the perch!' When she went to Bay House that summer the canary was seriously ill, 'dying, I fear,' said Jane. As a last resort she sent him to a lady called Mrs. Huxham, who, she said, 'is skilful in canaries'.

Little Charlotte, the servant left in charge at Cheyne Row, wrote to Jane on 7 August: 'I went to see the bird and he still very Bad and Mrs. Uxham wished me to give you her address as she would like to tell you all about it.'

And Mrs. Huxham did tell her all about it.

'Mrs. Huxham wrote me a touching effusion about "the Bird". From which I could only gather this—that if he lived he would live, and if he died he would die! and that meantime he "spent whole hours" (I should think not very happy ones) in Mrs. Huxham's "*bosom*"!! I hope he won't expect *us* to keep him in *our bosoms*, when he returns to his anxious family!'

A week later Mrs. Huxham wrote again. ' "The bird" is not only still living but "picking up",' Jane told Charlotte—' "washes and pecks himself"—for which the Heavens be duly praised! and Mrs. Huxham's *bosom*!'

Nero arrived in 1849, a present to Jane from Stauros Dilberoglue, a Greek whom she had met in Manchester. Telling this young man of the loss of her cat, she had said, idly, that she thought a dog would be better company—a little, well-behaved dog, she added, remembering her mother's little dog Shandy, who had been so much loved. To her surprise, Dilberoglue took her seriously: a small dog, he wrote, would shortly arrive at Cheyne Row. A little taken aback, she set about preparing the way.

'My dear,' she told Carlyle, 'it's borne in upon my mind that I am to have a dog!' She made a joke of it, but she was nervous of the dog's reception.

One evening a small fluffy black and white object was delivered at the front door by a railway guard.

'He is about the size of Shandy,' wrote Jane, 'but has long white silky hair hanging all about him—and over his eyes which are very large and black.' For the first few days Jane was on tenterhooks. 'I was afraid Mr. Carlyle would have found him a plague and ordered him about his business—and so he would if the dog had been noisy—but he is as good as dumb—*never* barks unless I make him do it in play—and then when Mr. C. comes in in bad humour the little beast never troubles its head but dances round him on its hind legs—till he comes *to* and feels quite grateful for his confidence in his good will. So he gives it raisins, of which it is very fond, one by one, and blows tobacco smoke in its face which it does not like so well—and calls it "you little villain" in a tone of great kindness.'

Jane was immensely relieved. Her delight in owning Nero had to be shared with all her friends.

'Oh, Lord! I forgot to tell you I have got a little dog,' she told Forster, 'and Mr. C. has accepted it with an amiability! To be sure, when he comes down gloomy in the morning, or comes in wearied from his walk, the infatuated little beast dances round him on its hind legs as I ought to do and can't; and he feels flattered and surprised by such unwonted capers to his honour and glory.'

And to her sympathetic friend Mary Russell she confided:

'*The* pleasantest fact of my life for a good while is, that I have got a beautiful little dog.' She hopes that she will not make a fool of herself with the creature, and repeats firmly that 'he is not of course, either so pretty or so clever as Shandy'. But 'I like him better,' she admits, 'than I should choose to show publicly.'

Nero's conquest of Carlyle pleased her: 'Not only has Mr. C. no temptation to "kick his foot thro' it", but seems getting quite fond of it and looks flattered when it musters the hardihood to leap on *his* knee.'

'My fear now,' she continues, 'is not that Mr. C. will put it away, but that I shall become the envy of surrounding dog-stealers! . . . Well! I can but get a chain to fasten it to my arm, and keep a sharp look out.'

One morning, only a week or two after his arrival, Nero disappeared.

'Yesterday, O heavens! I made my first experience of the strange, suddenly-struck-solitary, altogether ruined feeling of having lost one's dog,' wrote Jane. She had missed him, she said, just opposite the Wine Cooper's in Justice Walk, and the Cooper's apprentices, whom she employed from time to time on odd jobs, rushed off in search of the little dog. A man was caught, leading Nero by his collar: 'He said he had *found* the dog who was *losing* himself, and was bringing him after me!! and I would surely "give him a trifle for his *trouble*!" And I was coward enough to give him twopence,' she admitted, 'to rid Nero and myself of his dangerous proximity.'

This was only the first of several alarms. The following February, Nero was stolen 'for a whole day', wrote Jane; 'but escaped back to me on its own four legs. Mr. C. asked while it was a-missing: "What will you be inclined to give the dog-stealers, for bringing it back to you?" (dog-stealing being a regular trade here); and I answered passionately with a flood of tears "my whole half-year's allowance!" '

These calamities served to strengthen the bond between Jane and Nero. 'I have a little dog that I make more fuss about than beseems a sensible woman,' she told her sister-in-law. 'He walks with me, this creature, and sleeps with me and sits with me, so I am no longer alone any more than you are with your bairns. . . .'

Nero slept at the foot of her bed, and never disturbed her, she said, till she was ready to get up. 'It follows me like my shadow, and lies in my lap; and at meals, when animals are apt to be so trouble-some, it makes no sort of demonstration beyond standing on its hind legs!'

When Nero arrived at Cheyne Row the black cat imported to get rid of the mice was already installed. It accepted Nero as a friend, and the two animals became allies. 'Directly on the dining-room door opening', wrote Carlyle, Nero and the cat 'used to come waltzing in . . . in the height of joy, like Harlequin and Colum-bine, as I once heard remarked and did not forget.' From then, the little cat became known as Columbine.

Carlyle, staying at The Grange with the Ashburtons in January 1850, received the following missive:

'Dear Master,—I take the liberty to write to you myself (my mistress being out of the way of writing to you she says) that you may know Columbine and I are quite well, and play about as usual. There was no dinner yesterday to speak of; I had for my share only a piece of biscuit that might have been round the world; and if Columbine got anything at all, I didn't see it. I made a grab at one or two of the "small beings" on my mistress's plate; she called them "heralds of the morn"; but my mistress said, "Don't you wish you may get it?" and boxed my ears. I wasn't taken to walk on account of its being wet. And nobody came, but a man for "burial rate"; and my mistress gave him a rowing because she wasn't going to be buried here at all. Columbine and I don't mind where we are buried.'

The letter was continued later in the day:

'Dear Master,—My mistress brought my chain, and said "come along with me, while it shined and I could finish after". But she kept me so long in the London Library and other places, that I had to miss the post. An old gentleman in the omnibus took such notice of me! He looked at me a long time, and then turned to my mistress and said "Sharp, isn't he?" and my mistress was so good as to say "Oh yes!" And the old gentleman said again, "I knew it; easy to see that!" And he put his hand in his hind-pocket, and took out a whole biscuit, a sweet one, and gave it me in bits. I was quite sorry to part from him, he was such a good judge of dogs.'

The letter breaks off again, to be finished next morning.

'I left off last night, dear master, to be washed. This morning I have seen a note from you, which says you will come to-morrow. Columbine and I are extremely happy to hear it; for then there will be some dinner to come and go on. Being to see you so soon, no more at present from your

Obedient little dog,<br>Nero.'

Nero had not been at Cheyne Row two months, but already he was one of the family. Part Maltese terrier and part mongrel, he was, as the old gentleman noticed, 'sharp'; and 'in spite of Carlyle's disbelief,' said Jane, he was 'capable of a profound sentiment of affection'. He was very lively, and enjoyed long night walks with his master.

'Nero ran with me through the Brompton solitudes last night, merry as a maltman', wrote Carlyle; and on a long country walk, 'I took the little dog with me, which amused me by its happy gambollings.'

'The dog Nero,' he told his brother, 'goes out with (Jane) in the forenoon, out with *me* towards midnight (often about eleven) . . . and is the happiest of little dogs, poor wretch!' When Jane was unwell, Carlyle took him out in the mornings: 'The poor little *tatty* wretch, coursing after sparrows which he never catches—eager as a Californian *Digger*, and probably about as successful, often makes me reflect, and rather entertains me, in the Kensington field-lanes.'

But walks with Nero were not always so pleasantly philosophical.

'He lost me yesternight, the intolerable messin that he is. I was hurrying home from a long walk, full of reflections not pleasant. At the bottom of Cadogan Place eleven o'clock struck: time to hurry home for porridge. But the vermin was wanting; no whistle would bring him. I had to go back as far as Wilton Crescent. There the miserable quadruped appeared, and I nearly bullied the life out of him.'

But his master's wrath left Nero unmoved. 'He licked my milk-dish at home,' said Carlyle, 'with the same relish.' 'On the whole,' he continues angrily, 'he is a real nuisance and absurdity in this house.'

'Ach! we could have better spared a better dog,' cried Jane after another of these episodes: Carlyle returning from the walk and shouting 'Is that vermin come back?' 'Having received my horrified "No!"' said Jane, 'he hurried off again, and for twenty minutes I was in the agonies of one's dog lost, my heart beating up into my ears. At last I heard Mr. C.'s feet in the street; and, oh joy! heard him gollaring at something, and one knew what the little bad something was. . . .'

When Jane travelled, Nero travelled with her—except when she stayed with the Ashburtons. Her instinct told her that Nero would not be welcome. 'Love and a kiss to my poor wee dog', she wrote to Carlyle from The Grange. 'I missed him dreadfully at bedtime— But I see it was a particular Mercy of Heaven that I had the sense to resist *your* recommendation to fetch him with me.'

Lady Ashburton, hearing that Jane had a dog called Nero, addressed her whimsically as 'Agrippina', which must have pleased her, for she signed herself by this name when she wrote to Nero from Addiscombe in March 1850—

'My "poor orphan"! My dear good little dog! How are you? How do they use you? Above all, where did you sleep? Did they put you to bed by yourself in my empty room, or did you "cuddle in" with your surviving parent? Strange that amidst all my anxieties about you, it should never have struck me with whom you were to sleep; never once, until I was retiring to bed myself without you trotting at my heels! Still, darling, I am glad I did not take you with me. If there had been nothing else in it, the parrot alone was sufficient hindrance; she pops "all about"; and for certain you would have pulled her head off; and then it would have been all over with you and me.'

Four years later, she refused an invitation to 'rusticate' at Addiscombe while the Ashburtons were in the Highlands. 'In spite of the beauty and magnificence of that place, and all its belongings, I hate being there in the family's absence—am always afraid of my dog's making footmarks on the sofas or carpet.' Even after Lady Ashburton's death, when she was invited by Miss Baring to Bay House, she decided to leave Nero in Chelsea. 'Nero! Oh dear no!

Nero must "keep up his dignity" like his Mistress—must not go where he is *de trop*.'

Nero was a good traveller. When Jane took him to Sherborne he had to be smuggled into the carriage in a basket, for fear of being charged his fare. 'He gave me no trouble,' wrote Jane, 'kept himself hidden and motionless till the train started, and then looked out cautiously, as much as to say, "Are we safe?" '

But in July 1853, travelling to Liverpool on the way to Scotland, she paid 4*s*. for his ticket. 'I assure you, sir, he will lie quite quiet,' she said politely to her male fellow-passenger. 'He will not give you the slightest trouble.' 'I sincerely hope he will not!' was the disconcerting reply: an unpropitious start to the journey. But all went well, and 'The instant the door was opened at Liverpool', wrote Jane, 'Nero leapt out, tho' he had never stirred at any other stopping! The sense of that dog!! Nobody asked for his ticket,' she added, 'and I rather grudged the four shillings.'

They travelled on to Scotland, staying with Carlyle's brother John in Moffat. Here, climbing a mountain-side, Jane, with Nero at her heels, found herself stranded on a high ridge, with a precipice on either side. A cataract known as the Grey Mare's Tail was ahead. 'Nero grew quite frightened, and pressed against my legs; and when we came close in front of the waterfall, he stretched out his neck at it from under my petticoats, and then barked furiously.' 'I grew, for the first time in my life that I remember of, frightened, physically frightened. . . .' She had taken a double dose of morphia the night before, and now she felt light-headed. 'To go back on my hands and knees as I had come up was impossible; my only chance was to look at the grass under my face, and toil on till John should see me. I tried to call to him, but my tongue stuck fast and dry to the roof of my mouth; Nero barking with terror, and keeping close to my head, still further confused me.'

Fortunately, John Carlyle recognized her danger, and succeeded in reaching her and steering her to safety. 'In my life I was never so thankful,' she said, 'as when I found myself at the bottom of that hill with a glass of water to drink.' Even Nero was forgotten, in her relief.

After being away for four weeks she wrote announcing the day of her return and asking her husband to meet her at Euston Square station. 'Nero,' she adds, 'bids me say, not to feel hurt should he show little joy at seeing you, as his digestion is all deranged since he has been here, with the constant crumbs of "suet and plums" that fall to his share. When I came from Church today, tho' it had been the first hour he had been separated from me since we left home together, he could hardly raise a jump.'

Nero's welcomes after a parting always warmed Jane's heart and she was unashamedly disappointed when her reception was not enthusiastic.

'Nero was awoke out of a sound sleep by my rap', she wrote on coming home from Addiscombe; 'and came to the door yawning and stretching himself, and did not give even one bark; just looked, as much as to say, "Oh, you are there again, are you? well, I was doing quite nicely with Ann". So there was not even "a dog glad at my home-coming!" '

In the summer of 1857 she went to Scotland, leaving Nero at Cheyne Row with his master. Her letters contain messages to him— 'a kiss to Nero'; 'Be kind to Nero'; and when she announced the time of her return, 'Tell Nero'. But when she arrived, 'I am shocked', she wrote, 'to have to confess that Nero was far from showing the enthusiasm "England expected" of him! He knew me quite well, but took me very coolly indeed. Ann said he had just been sleeping. Let us hope he was in a state of indigestion, in which dogs are not capable of being more amiable than their owners.'

In a household where indigestion was synonymous with bad temper it was natural that Nero's 'interior' should be thought to influence his state of mind. Jane watched over his health with as much care as if he were a child. Just as she raged at Carlyle for eating crystallized greengages at Lady Ashburton's she inveighed against 'everyone stuffing (Nero) with dainties, out of kindness'.

'When I say I am well, it means also Nero is well; he is part and parcel of myself', she wrote. He was her constant companion—'the chief comfort of my life—night and day he never leaves me, and it is something, I can tell you, to have such a bit of live cheerfulness always beside one'.

She flattered herself that Nero returned her affection.

'Going down into the kitchen the morning after my return from Sherborne, I spoke to the white cat, in common politeness, and even stroked her', she wrote to Carlyle in 1852; 'whereupon the jealousy of Nero rose to a pitch. He snapped and barked at me, then flew at the cat quite savage. I "felt it my duty" to box his ears. He stood a moment as if taking his resolution; then rushed up the kitchen stairs; and, as it afterward appeared, out of the house! For, in ten minutes or so, a woman came to the front door with master Nero in her arms; and said she had met him running up Cook's grounds, and was afraid he "would go and lose himself!" He would take no notice of *me* for several hours after!' 'And yet', she added, 'he had never read "George-Sand Novels", that dog, or any sort of Novels!'

To Jane this display of jealousy was entrancing; often she was to write of Nero as if he were human.

'The clock struck twelve', she wrote to Carlyle, 'and Nero, with his usual good sense, insisted on my going to bed; he had gone half an hour before by himself, and established himself under the bed-clothes; but he returned at twelve and jumped till I rose and followed him.'

'I could stand the creature's loss now less than ever', she wrote in 1852, after Nero had disappeared while his mistress was in the nursery-man's buying plants. 'After looking all about for him, I hurried back home and when the door was opened he bounded into my arms. Ann said "he got a lady to knock at the door for him!"' 'The half hour's fright', she added, 'had given me what Ann called "quite a turn".'

Her feelings for Nero made her sympathetic to other dog-lovers. 'By the way, how is Mary's blessed Tearem?' she asked Helen Welsh. 'Her attachment to that I must say not very lovely dog was quite beautiful, so superior to both abuse and ridicule.' But she could not bear to see a dog spoiled. Though it pleased her to invest Nero with human characteristics, he was treated as a dog; his diet was scraps and biscuit. She was shocked, when lunching at a restaurant called Grange's, to see a dog seated on a chair at the next table, devouring plateful after plateful of cakes. 'His companion, who was treating him, finally snatched up a large pound-cake, cut it into junks, and handed him one after another on the point of a knife, till that also had gone *ad plura*.'

'By the way,' she continued, 'it must have been a curious sight for the starved beggars, who hang about the doors of such places, to see a dog make away with as much cake in five minutes as would have kept them in bread for a week, or weeks!' 'I should like to know the name of the "gentleman as belonged to that dog",' she said. 'Should one find him some other day maintaining in Parliament that "all goes well", it would throw some light on the worth of his opinion to know that his dog may have as much pound-cake at Grange's as it likes to eat!'

Dogs are said to reflect the characteristics of their owners, and something of Jane may perhaps have found its way into Nero, who was an original and intrepid character. Carlyle might lose his temper, declare 'that vermin' to be 'a real nuisance and absurdity in this house'; but there was something disarming about the little beast which always made him relent.

Nero seemed to bear a charmed life. 'He has had another escape, that dog!' wrote Jane in March 1850. She had been in bed with a cold, and Nero, missing his morning walk, was at a loose end. 'Imagine', wrote his fond mistress, 'Imagine his taking it into his head that he could *fly*—like the birds—if he tried! and actually trying it—out at the Library window! For a first attempt his success was not so bad; for he fairly cleared the area spikes—and tho' he *did* plash down on the pavement at the feet of an astonished Boy he broke no bones, was only quite *stunned*. He gave us a horrid fright however.' It was after breakfast, and he had been standing in the open window, watching the birds—one of his chief delights—while Elizabeth was 'dusting out' for Mr. C. 'Lying in my bed', wrote Jane, 'I heard thro' the deal partition Elizabeth scream; "Oh God! oh Nero!" and rush downstairs like a strong wind out at the street door. I sat up in bed aghast—waiting with a feeling as of the Heavens falling till I heard her reascending the stairs and then I sprang to meet her in my night shift. She was white as a sheet, ready to faint—could just say; "Oh *take* him!" the dog's *body* lay on her arm! "Is he killed?" I asked with terrible self-possession. "Not quite—I think, all *but!*"

'Mr. C. came down from his bedroom with his chin all over soap and asked "has anything happened to Nero?" "Oh Sir he *must* have broken *all* his legs, he leapt out at *your* window!" "God bless me!" said Mr. C. and returned to his shaving. I sat down on the floor and laid my insensible dog over my knees, but could see no *breakage*— only a stun. So I took him to bed with me—*under* the clothes— and in an hour's time he was as brisk and active as ever.'

Some nine years later she had to face a worse disaster. The maid, Charlotte, had taken Nero out shopping. Charlotte was devoted to Jane's dog, who had kept her company the summer before when the Carlyles were at Bay House. She was young and lively, and played with Nero whenever Jane was ill; and if she ran to the shops Nero ran with her. On this fateful evening Jane opened the door to find Charlotte in floods of tears with Nero in her arms, 'all crumpled together like a crushed spider, and his poor little eyes protruding and fixedly staring in his head!' He had been run over. 'A butcher's cart, driving furiously round a sharp corner', had passed over his throat. He was not dead; but when Jane placed him gently on the floor he toppled over 'quite stiff and unconscious'. Once again she mastered her feelings—'Charlotte was so distressed,' she said, 'and really could not have helped it'.

'I put him in a warm bath,' she said, 'and afterwards wrapped him warmly and laid him on a pillow, and left him, without much hope of finding him alive in the morning. But in the morning he still breathed, though incapable of any movement; but he swallowed some warm milk I put into his mouth. About midday I was saying aloud "Poor dog! poor little Nero!" when I saw the bit tail trying to wag itself! and after that, I had good hopes.'

Nero recovered, 'but it was ten days before he was able to raise a bark, his first attempt was like the scream of an infant'. His recovery seemed miraculous—'a revelation,' said Jane, 'of the strength of the throat of a dog'.

C.A.H.–K

But the recovery was not complete: Nero was never the same. He grew languid and asthmatic. 'I have made him a little red cloak', Jane wrote later that autumn, 'and he keeps the house with me.' The Carlyles spent Christmas at The Grange, and Jane returned 'with sickening apprehension'. For the first time in eleven years there was no welcoming bark. 'Was he really dead then? No! strange to say, he was actually a little better and had run up the kitchen stairs to welcome me as usual; but there he had been arrested by a paroxysm of coughing, and the more he tried to show his joy the more he could not do it.'

This pathetic picture is the last: Nero had not much longer to live. 'Mr. C.,' said Jane, 'keeps insisting on "a little prussic acid" for him!' She could not bear the thought; and even Carlyle had his moments of sentiment. 'Poor little fellow!' Jane heard him saying in the garden, 'I declare I am heartily sorry for you! If I could make you young again, upon my soul I would!'

In the end, Jane gave way: on 1 February 1860, she called on her doctor, Mr. Barnes, and asked him with tears streaming down her face, to come and put an end to Nero's sufferings.

'My dear good Mr. Barnes,' she wrote next day, 'I cannot put into words how much I feel your kindness. It was such a kind thing to do! and so kindly done! My gratitude to you will be as long as my life, for shall I not, as long as I live, remember that poor little Dog?

'Oh don't think me absurd—*you*—for caring so much about a dog! Nobody but myself can have any idea what that little creature has been in my life! My inseparable Companion during eleven years, ever doing *his* little best to keep me from feeling sad and lonely! Docile, affectionate, loyal up to his last hour, when weak and full of pain he *offered to go with me*, seeing my bonnet on; and came panting to welcome me on my return! and the reward I gave him—the only reward I *could* or *ought* to give him—to such a pass had things come —was, ten minutes after, to give him up to be poisoned!

'I thought it not unlikely you would call today—because your coming today would be of a piece with the rest of your goodness to me. Nevertheless I went out for a lonely drive. I couldn't bear myself in the house, where everything I looked at reminded me of yesterday. And I wouldn't be at home for visitors, to criticise my swollen eyes and smile at grief "about a dog!" and besides, suppose *you* came, I wished to *not* treat you to more tears, of which you had had too much—and today I couldn't for my life have seen you without crying dreadfully.'

The death of Nero shook the whole household. 'Mr. C.,' said Jane, 'couldn't have reproached me (for wasting so much feeling on a dog), for he himself was in tears at the poor little thing's end! and his own heart was (as he phrased it) "unexpectedly and distractedly torn to pieces with it!" As for Charlotte, she went about for three days after with her face all swollen and red with weeping. But on the fourth day,' Jane was obliged to add, 'she got back her good looks and gay spirits; and much sooner, Mr. C. had got to speak of "poor Nero" composedly enough.'

For Jane, the grief was not so quickly overcome. She spoke of 'a constantly recurring blank'; she even speculated about Nero's immortality. 'What is become of that little, beautiful, graceful *Life*, so full of love and loyalty and sense of duty, up to the last minute that it animated the body of that little dog?' And she was grateful to her aunt Grace Welsh, who 'actually gave me a reference to certain verses in *Romans* which *seemed* to warrant my belief in the immortality of animal life as well as human'. 'One thing is sure, however,' she concluded, 'my little dog is buried at the top of our garden; and I grieve for him as if he had been my little human child.'

## CHAPTER NINE

# *Money*

'DID you fill up the Income Tax paper?' Jane inquired anxiously of her husband. 'If you didn't, you must do it yet—even if *after* the appointed time, or there will be another hundred pounds or two clapped on to the Tax! and I shall have to *"appeal"* again. . . .'

Unlike most Victorian wives, who were kept in ignorance of the amount, and often even the source, of their husbands' incomes, Jane knew every detail of the finances of Cheyne Row; indeed, by mutual agreement, she was in charge of them.

Carlyle was frugal by upbringing and habit, but generous by nature: if he bought Jane a present, it was an expensive one. 'Carlyle has just one rule in buying anything,' said Jane, 'to buy what is best that is *dearest*.' And he hated to be bothered with financial problems: he made his wife an allowance, and there was what she called a 'money row' if she had to go to him for more. This was hard, for she was, as he himself said, 'the best of housewives'. Thrifty by nature, she enjoyed a good haggle if it was successful (and it generally was); she kept scrupulous accounts, and was careful of every penny.

In 1858, a builder charged £5. 7s. 6d. for putting in a new grate in the attic study. 'Don't trouble yourself about B——', wrote Carlyle, 'I will pay him.' But Jane was determined to trouble herself. She sent for an ironmonger from the King's Road, and asked him to estimate the cost of the work. 'He said *he* should have considered himself well paid with 30s.; but B. being farther off and more expensive, he thought I might offer £2. 15s—not more.' She accordingly offered this sum; 'or I would let the matter be settled by arbitration; or he might prosecute me for the whole amount in the County Court'.

After two hours' argument with the foreman, sent to look at the job, Jane reluctantly settled for £3. 10s. She was upset: it was '15/- more than I had decided to pay'; and 'for hours I seemed to have got St Vitus's dance in all my veins—and to fix my attention was impossible'. But she had won her point, shown that she would not be overcharged; and no doubt the foreman was tired after the interview, too.

When she was away from home the current servant was expected to keep accounts. Coming back in 1845, Jane wrote:

'The economical department (is) in a very backward state, but not confused, for it is as clear as day that not a single bill has been paid since I left. Helen seems to have had four pounds ten for the incidental expenses, which I shall inclose her account of . . . and there is a national debt to the butcher, baker, and milkman, amounting to about five pounds. So that the housekeeping, during my absence, has been carried on at some six or seven shillings a week less than if I had been at home, which is all as it should be, for I defy three people to live as we do on less than thirty shillings a week.'

A month later she was reluctantly forced to apply to Carlyle for money: she did this in a letter, while he was still safely in Scotland. He had left her £30 when he went away. ' "The thirty pounds

I left done already?" ' she imagined him asking. ' "No, not done absolutely, but near it; and yet my living has been as moderate as well could be." It is so provoking,' she exclaims, 'when I wanted so much to have been praised for my economy, to have to say instead, you must bring more money. But just take the trouble to see how it has gone, without any mention of victuals at all.

| | £ | | |
|---|---|---|---|
| 'Your debt to clear off | 4 | 18 | 6 |
| 'Water-rate | 0 | 6 | 6 |
| 'Church-rate | 0 | 11 | 3 |
| 'Rent | 8 | 15 | 0 |
| 'Aldin's quarter's account | 5 | 8 | 0 |
| 'Taxes | 3 | 2 | $2\frac{1}{2}$ |
| 'To Helen of Wages | 1 | 0 | 0 |
| | £24 | 1 | $5\frac{1}{2}$' |

With this account she enclosed all the receipts. Jane was business-like.

In 1842, Income Tax, which had been levied during the Napoleonic Wars and repealed in 1816, was reintroduced by Sir Robert Peel. In 1855 it was raised to 1*s.* 4*d.* in the £—double what it had been previously—and became a serious problem.

Carlyle received a demand for tax on his last three years' earnings, which he had assessed in 1854 as averaging £150 a year. The demand came at an unfortunate time, for he had published nothing for several years. True, he had saved about £2,000, which was deposited in a Dumfries bank; and Jane received an income of £150 from Craigenputtock, which, with the royalties he was still receiving on *The French Revolution* and *Cromwell* provided enough for their needs. But the tax demand was a blow.

A writer's earnings vary from year to year, Carlyle's more than most. His income at this time fluctuated between £800, which he earned in 1847, and something under £150 for the years between 1848 and 1855. The writing of his major works was so intense and exhausting a struggle that at the finish of a book he was incapable of putting his mind to another for months, even years.

'For above two years now,' he wrote in 1848, 'I have been as good as totally idle, composedly lying *fallow*. It is frightful to think of! After getting out of '*Cromwell*', my whole being seemed to say, more sulkily, more weariedly than ever before, "What good is it?' " 'Thou must gird up thy loins again', he urges himself, 'and work another stroke or two before thou die.'

He had no wish for wealth—'I authentically feel indifferent to money, would not go this way or that to gain more money.' But he had experienced poverty, and could not bear the petty aggravations of day-to-day economy; nor could he stand argument about money. In 1855 he was making Jane an allowance of £50 a quarter. It was she who paid the bills—'Went in an omnibus to Coutts's Bank', she wrote on 1 July 1856, 'to pay my rent. Returned on foot, stopping in Pall Mall to pay the Fire Insurance. "How provoking it is," I said to the man, "to be paying all this money every year, when one never has anything burnt." "Well, Ma'am," said the man, "you can set fire to your house, and see how you like it!" '

She also paid, as we have seen, the rates and taxes. And in November 1855, in response to their exhorbitant demand, she made up her mind to beard the Commissioners of Inland Revenue.

It was the only thing to do. 'If Mr. C. should go,' she wrote in her journal, 'he would run his head against some post in his impatience; and besides, for me, when it is over it will be over, whereas he would not get the better of it for twelve months—if ever at all.'

She was determined to make the fight; but she was also determined to be a martyr. She worked herself into a fever of nerves about the prospective interview: it was after all, she realized belatedly, a most unsuitable mission for a woman to undertake.

Carlyle became aware of her state of mind. 'Mr. C. said "the voice of honour seemed to call on him to go himself". But either it did not call loud enough,' said Jane, 'or he would not listen.' She was filled with self-pity. 'It was with feeling like the ghost of a dead dog, that I rose and drank my coffee, and started for Kensington.'

She went in a cab, 'to save my breath for appealing'.

The tax office, number 30 Hornton Street, Kensington, was a dreary-looking private house. The door was opened by a dirty servant, who told Jane to walk upstairs and wait: the Commissioners would not be there for half an hour.

'There were already some half-score of men assembled in the waiting-room,' she said, 'among whom I saw the man who cleans our clocks, and a young Apothecary of Cheyne Walk.' She had the impression that no one in the room except these two could possibly have been suspected of earning as much as a hundred a year. After a long, depressing vigil, while 'men trooped in by twos and threes' —and eventually, to her relief, three other females, all extremely worried-looking—the Commissioners' clerk thrust his head round a small door, and called 'First come lady!' (an unexpected piece of chivalry)—and Jane thankfully stepped into the unknown.

She was led into a dim room where three men sat round a table spread with papers. 'One held a pen ready over an open ledger, another was taking snuff, and had taken still worse in his time, to judge by his shaky, clayed appearance. The third, who was plainly the cock of that dungheap, was sitting for Rhadamanthus—a Rhadamanthus without justice.

' "Name," said the horned-owl-looking individual holding the pen. "Carlyle." "What?" "Carlyle." Seeing he still looked dubious, I spelt it for him.

' "Ha!" cried Rhadamanthus, a big, bloodless-faced, insolent-looking fellow. "What is this? Why is Mr. Carlyle not come himself? Didn't he get a letter ordering him to appear?" '

Jane replied coldly that she had been 'told by one of your fellow Commissioners that Mr. Carlyle's personal appearance was not indispensable'.

' "Huffgh! Huffgh! What does Mr. Carlyle mean by saying he has no fixed income from his writings, when he himself fixed it at a hundred and fifty?"

' "It means, sir, that, in ceasing to write, one ceases to be paid for writing, and Mr. Carlyle has published nothing for several years." '

Jane produced Chapman and Hall's statement to prove this. Rhadamanthus snorted.

' "What am I to make of that? Huffgh! We should have Mr. Carlyle here to swear to this before we believe it."

' "If a gentleman's word of honour written at the bottom of that paper is not enough," retorted Jane, "you can put me on my oath: I am ready to swear to it."

' "You! you indeed! No, no, we can do nothing with your oath."

' "But sir, I understand my husband's affairs fully, better than he does himself."

' "That I can well believe; but we can make nothing of this," flinging my document contemptuously on the table. The horned owl picked it up, glanced over it . . . then handed it back to him, saying deprecatingly: "But sir, this is a very plain statement."

' "Then what has Mr. Carlyle to live upon? You don't tell me he lives on that?" pointing to the document.

' "Heaven forbid, sir! But I am not here to explain what Mr. Carlyle has to live on, only to declare his income from literature during the last three years."

' "True, true!" mumbled the not-most-important voice at my elbow. "Mr. Carlyle, I believe, has landed income." "Of which," said I haughtily, for my spirit was up, "I have fortunately no account to render in this kingdom and to this board." '

By this time Rhadamanthus evidently realized that Jane was not to be browbeaten. He decided to bring the interview to an end.

' "Take off fifty pounds, say a hundred—take off a hundred pounds," said Rhadamanthus to the horned owl. "If we write Mr. Carlyle down a hundred and fifty he has no reason to complain, I think. There, you may go. Mr. Carlyle has no reason to complain."

'On stepping out,' Jane added, 'my first thought was, what a mercy Carlyle didn't come himself!'

She had triumphed; but she felt no sense of victory, only relief that the unpleasant experience was over.

In 1857, Peel's high taxation was reduced; but Jane's memory of her interview with the Commissioners lingered: the thought of it was like a bad dream, when she begged her husband, seven years later, not to risk another 'appeal'.

In 1855, the year of the doubled income tax, food prices also rose. Jane was faced with a serious financial crisis. Her allowance would no longer go round. She lay sleepless, pondering how to broach the subject without a scene. On previous occasions, Carlyle had staved her off with loud words, she said, accusing her of pestering his life out about money, and declaring that his soul was sick with hearing about it. Allowing for her artistic exaggeration, it seems fairly clear that, faced with a new demand for money, Carlyle would be upset.

Once again, Jane decided that the safest course would be to write, not speak, even though they were in the same house. She would prepare a statement on the lines of a Parliamentary Budget, in the hope that Carlyle's rage would be overcome by his appreciation of her manner of presenting the unpalatable facts.

On 12 February 1855, he received a packet containing several pages in Jane's handwriting. The missive was entitled 'Budget of a *Femme Incomprise*'.

'I dont choose to *speak* again on the *money question!*' she begins, provocatively enough. 'The replies from the Noble Lord are unfair and unkind and little to the purpose.' She goes on:

'You don't understand why the allowance which sufficed in former years no longer suffices. That is what I would explain to the Noble Lord if he would but—what shall I say?—*keep his temper*.'

The beginning of her embarrassments, she continues, was the miserable 'earthquake' of 1852–3 when the soundproof study was built. 'There was an incessant recurrence of small incidental expenses, during all that period, through which I found myself in September gone a year, ten pounds behind, instead of having some pounds saved up towards the winter's coals. I could have worked round "out of that", however, in the course of time, if habits of *unpinched* housekeeping had not been long taken by you as well as myself. . . .'

The fact was that since Carlyle had become a literary lion, he and Jane were inevitably keeping up more state than in their first years at Cheyne Row. Geraldine Jewsbury remarked that no one who visited the Carlyles could tell whether they were poor or rich. This was largely due to Jane's cleverness and energy: but by now they were in the habit of visiting at great houses, and it was inevitable that their own way of life should, however imperceptibly, have grown easier, more in keeping with their position. Carlyle kept a horse;

they travelled; Jane was always well dressed; indeed, according to Froude, 'there was much curiosity among their friends to know how the establishment was supported'.

'I will show the Noble Lord,' Jane continued, 'with his permission, what the new current expenses are, and to what they amount per annum. ("Hear, hear!" and cries of "Be brief!")

'1. We have a servant of a higher grade than we ever ventured on before. Anne's wages are 16 pounds a year; Fanny's were 13. Most of the others had twelve; and Anne never dreams of being other than *well fed*. The others *scrambled* for their living out of ours. Her regular meat dinner at one o'clock, regular allowance of butter, etc., adds at least three pounds a year to the year's bills. But she plagues us with no fits of illness nor of drunkenness, no *warnings* nor complainings . . . Anne is the last item I should vote for retrenching in.'

'2. We have now gas and water "laid on", both producing admirable results.'

But she points out that they are now paying £1. 16s. per annum for their running water, plus a shilling to the turncock, whereas in the old days of the pump they only paid 4d. a week to the water-carrier. The difference, she works out (inaccurately) is 'nineteen shillings and fourpence'.

As for the gas-light, she reckons that it is costing at least 15s. more than the few 6d. boxes of lights used in the kitchen before the gas was laid on. 'These two excellent innovations, then, increase the yearly expenditure by one pound fourteen shillings and fourpence—a trifle to speak of; but you, my Lord, born and bred in Scotland, must know well the proverb, "Every little mak's a mickle."'

'3. *We are higher taxed*. Within the last eighteen months there has been added to the Lighting, Pavement, and Improvement Rate ten shillings yearly, to the Poor Rate one pound, to the sewer rate ten shillings; and now the doubled Income Tax makes a difference of £5. 16s. 8d. yearly, which sums, added together, amount to a difference of £7. 16s. 8d. yearly, on taxes which already amounted to £17. 12s. 8d.'

'4. Provisions of all sorts are higher priced than in former years.

Four shillings a week for bread, instead of two shillings and sixpence, makes at the year's end a difference of £3. 18s. Butter has kept all the year round 2d. a pound dearer than I ever knew it. On the quantity we use—two pounds and a half per week "quite reg'lar'— there is a difference of 21/- 8d. by the year. Butcher's meat is a penny a pound dearer. At the rate of a pound and a half a day, *bones* included—no exhorbitant allowance for three people—the difference on that at the year's end would be £2. 5s. 6d. Coals, which had been for some years at 21s. per ton, cost this year 26s., last year 29s., bought judiciously, too. If I had to pay 50s. a ton for them, as some housewives had to, God knows what would have become of me. (Passionate cries of "Question! question!") We burn, or used to burn—I am afraid they are going faster this winter—twelve tons, one year with another.'

Candles, she goes on, have also gone up: they are 1s. a lb. instead of 10d.; and—because Carlyle will sit up so late—they burn 3 lb. in nine days. Bacon, soap, potatoes have all gone up—'potatoes at the cheapest, a penny a pound, instead of three pounds for 2d. We use three pounds of potatoes in two days' meals,' she adds. 'Who could imagine that at the year's end that makes a difference of 15/2 on one's mere potatoes?'

The only items which Jane did not pay for were wines and spirits—Carlyle's responsibility—and the winter's butter. 'Ever since we have been in London *you* have, in the handsomest manner, paid the winter's butter with *your own money*, though it was not in the bond. And this gentlemanlike proceeding on your part, till the butter became uneatable, was a good two pounds saved me,' said Jane, adding this to her sum of extra expenses.

| | | | |
|---|---|---|---|
| '1. Rise on servant | £6 | 0 | 0 |
| '2. Rise on light and water | 1 | 14 | 0 |
| '3. On Taxes | 7 | 16 | 8 |
| '4. On provisions | 12 | 0 | 0 |
| '5. Cessation of butter | 2 | 0 | 0 |
| | £29 | 10 | 8' |

'My calculation,' she adds, 'will be found quite correct, though I am not strong in arithmetic. I have *thochtered* all this well in my head, and *indignation* makes a sort of arithmetic, as well as verses.'

'Do you finally understand,' she asks, 'why the allowance which sufficed formerly no longer suffices, and pity my difficulties instead of being angry at them?'

But she would not leave the problem unsolved. With meticulous care she now set herself to work out how to raise the extra £29 without drawing on Carlyle's income. She is prepared, she says, to forgo his handsome Christmas and birthday presents, his New Year present—'Give me nothing; neither money nor money's worth,' she begs him. She offers to cut down her dress allowance from £25 a year to £15. 'A silk dress, a splendid dressing gown, "a milliner's bonnet" the less; what signifies that at my age? Nothing!' she declares bravely.

Having prepared the way, she now delivers the final shock. 'There only remains to disclose the actual state of the exchequer. It is as empty as a drum. (Sensation.)

'If I was a man,' she cries, 'I might fling the gauntlet to Society, join with a few brave fellows, and "rob a diligence". But my sex kind o' debars from that.' She cannot resist a dig at Lady Ashburton.

'Mercy! to think there are women—your friend Lady A., for example (*"Rumeurs!"* Sensation)—I say for *example*; who spend not merely the additamental pounds I must make such a pother about, but *four times my whole income* in the *ball* of one night, and none the worse for it, nor anyone the better.'

Signing herself, 'Your obedient humble servant, Jane Welsh Carlyle', she folded and sealed her Budget, left it on Carlyle's table while he was out in the garden smoking, and waited anxiously for his response.

As she had hoped, he was pleased and amused by her ingenuity, and wrote at the bottom of the last page:

'Excellent, my dear clever Goody, thriftiest, wittiest, and cleverest of women. I will set thee up again to a certainty, and thy £30 more shall be granted, thy bits of debts paid, and thy will be done. T.C.'

He was true to his word: the 'bits of debts' were promptly settled, and the Budget put away with a note to the effect that Jane's quarterly income was in future to be £58.

This was a mercy, for the following year prices rose again.

'Everything is now changed and changing with furious rapidity in this country', Carlyle wrote to his brother Alexander, who had emigrated to Canada. 'A great increase of luxury is coming over all ranks; prices of everything very nearly *doubled* (13*d*. per lb. for butter, 1*d*. each for eggs, and all in proportion), so that farmers prosper amazingly.'

Carlyle had at last begun to feel his way into the first volume of *Frederick the Great*, after many false starts: the need to earn perhaps acted as an extra incentive; for in May 1856 he wrote to his sister Mrs. Aitken, 'I believe I shall have to get to Press this very Autumn (or sooner) with the First Half of my wretched Book.' For over three years he had been reading and making notes. 'I shall *have* to sort these accumulated rubbish mounds,' he said, 'and cut my way thro' them better or worse. . . .'

There was also to be a collected edition of his works—'fourteen or fifteen volumes, 6/- per volume, and very respectable paper and print. This is very welcome for several reasons, first of all that it will yield a little fraction of *payment* again (more than I ever got before perhaps) after so long an interval.'

Chapman, his publisher, was 'a stingy, close-fisted kind of fellow'; but Carlyle succeeded in striking a satisfactory bargain with him for the *Collected Works*, and agreed to try and finish the first volume of *Frederick* ('the printer chasing me') that autumn. It was not till the following summer, however, that he was able to write 'I am fairly *printing* that unspeakable New Book; 150 pages of it *off my hands* forevermore.'

By June 1858 he had finished the first two volumes, and on their publication he was paid £2,800, the largest sum he had ever received for his writing.

' "Frederick" ', he was soon to note, 'has been considerably more read than usual with Books of mine.'

From now, the Carlyles' financial situation was eased. Worries of health, temperament, and the perpetual strain of living 'in the valley of the shadow of "Frederick",' oppressed them; but they were freed from the need to economize. There was little sign, in their way of life, that they were now comfortably off; but there had been little sign, in their days of poverty, that money was scarce. Jane continued to keep her careful accounts, and to complain if the servants were extravagant: she could not bear to think of money or food being wasted.

In December 1865—four months before her death—she wrote to the Ashburtons' gardener in Hampshire, begging him to cut down the supplies of fruit and flowers he sent every week to Cheyne Row.

'I am sure Mr. Cross you will think me lost to a sense of my own interest,' she writes, 'when you find the purport of this note is to prohibit *the hamper*!—at least partially; that is, two weeks out of the three!

'If I had unlimited shillings (as many people have) I should think these flowers, *alone*, so beautiful, and in such perfect preservation, well worth the carriage of the whole hamper, which has grown to be from four to five shillings a time! But as it is, I feel that hamper, just now, a sort of *luxury* that I ought not to indulge myself in!

'For you see, the flowers are "*all to myself*" (as the children say). Mr. C. has no taste for them . . . and is constantly assuring me when he sees me arranging them that *he* "wouldn't give a brass farthing for a whole cartload of them!!!"

'Of the vegetables I may almost say the same—that these are "all to myself"! Now that Mr. C. has got *old* potatoes again, he will eat no other vegetables whatever.'

These weekly hampers of garden produce, first from Addiscombe and then from Hampshire, were sent as a gift from the second Lady Ashburton, since Jane's bad illness in 1864. It was characteristic of Jane to count the cost of carriage and resent the waste of good vegetables. It does not seem to have occurred to her that these might have been eaten up in the kitchen.

She loved flowers. Most women would have rejoiced to have a fresh supply of country flowers every week; but to Jane this was unnecessary extravagance. She could keep her flowers alive 'amazingly long', she said—'*when I am put to it!*' And she made it clear that she preferred to be 'put to it' rather than know that any sort of waste was going on.

During the 1860's there were only two signs that the Carlyles were better off. In October 1864 Carlyle bought his wife a brougham. This had been considered for a long time, but it was only after Jane's accident and serious illness that Carlyle made the move.

'I have now set up a nice little Brougham', Jane wrote to Mary Russell, 'all to myself, with a smart grey horse and an elderly driver (in Mr. C.'s old brown surtout!).' She adds that the livery-stable man 'who has kept Mr. C.'s horse these dozen years', considered it a great bargain. 'Sixty pounds, and perfectly new, and handsome in a plain way.' This equipage, with its dark-blue morocco and cloth inside, was a great joy to Jane, and she drove out in it daily, as befitted the wife of a famous man.

The second sign of prosperity was not so welcome to Jane. In 1860 she was obliged by ill health to increase her domestic staff.

'So now I am mistress of *two* servants,' she cried, '—and ready to hang myself!'

CHAPTER TEN

# *The Garden*

ALTHOUGH Chelsea was still a riverside village, separated from
Kensington by fields and hawthorn-bordered lanes, the garden
at Cheyne Row was a typical town garden—an oblong patch,
79 feet by 20 feet, surrounded by high brick walls. After the farm-
lands and moors of Craigenputtock it must have seemed cramped
indeed, and hardly worth cultivating. Nevertheless, Carlyle determined to make use of the ground to grow fruit and vegetables; and
only a few days after they arrived he set to work to clear the weeds
which rampaged over everything, and give the garden 'a clean face'.
The upper soil was thin with a gravelly subsoil, but fruit-trees had
managed to thrust their roots down far enough to survive; and the
mulberry-trees in neighbouring gardens, together with the fine
walnut tree which pleased Jane by providing sixpennyworth of nuts,

were probably part of a seventeenth century orchard. Shrewsbury
House, built in 1543 and demolished in 1813, had owned the land
to the south and south-east, and the Tudor wall of this estate ran
along the end of the Carlyles' garden.

'Nothing I know of is more lasting than a well made brick,' said
Carlyle: 'we have them here, at the head of this garden . . . in
their third or fourth century (Henry VIII's time, I am told), and
still perfect in every particular.'

Gardening was good exercise, and after writing all the morning
Carlyle often dug till dinner time at four. By the end of that first
summer he and Jane could look out on a tidy garden: marigolds
were blooming, the sickly roses were freed of weeds, and the
vines in full leaf with a prospect of several bunches of grapes;
the birds, gobbling mulberries, dropped crimson splashes over
the grass. The Carlyles were enchanted by their *rus in urbe*, and
Thomas wrote to his sister Jean, 'We have not yet ceased to
admire the union of quietness, and freshness of air, and the
outlook into green trees (Plum trees, Walnuts, even Mulberries,
they say), with the close neighbourhood of the noisiest Babylon
that ever raged and *fumed* (with coal smoke) on the face of this
Planet.'

In the spring, digging was resumed, and in April Carlyle reported, 'Our piece of garden is all dug, and has wall-flower blossoms,
plum blossoms, vines budding, and much *spearmint*.'

'The crop of turnips flourishes amazingly,' he announced next
year. 'Beans, mignonette, and all the rest are growing and stretching
in the most vagrant manner'; and one is reminded of Mr. Holbrook's
garden in 'Cranford' where 'roses and currant-bushes touched each
other, and where the feathery asparagus formed a pretty background
to the pinks and gillyflowers'. Years later Jane was to assure Lady
Ashburton's gardener that 'Mr. C. does not know a myrtle from a
nettle!' so it seems likely that it was Carlyle who grew the vegetables
and Jane the flowers.

In spite of Jane's firm belief that raw fruit was of no use but to
give people a colic, Carlyle cherished his fruit-trees, and was apt to
pluck and eat his own green pears 'as a melancholy distraction' (and

with unfortunate results) while he strolled and pondered, in dressing-gown and straw hat.

His brother Alexander sent him an axe and a sickle. 'The sickle', he wrote, 'hangs on a branch of our old scrag of a cherry tree (which grows large quantities of cherries, mostly eaten by sparrows); I mow the grass with it, hew down the superfluous vine-branches, and many a time thank poor Alick's brotherliness.' Seven years later the axe was used to cut down the old cherry and pear-trees which had ceased to bear, and Carlyle planted three new fruit-trees in his 'poor sooty patch of a garden'. They would take time to settle down, he said: '*one* pear, and *one* cherry, seem to be all our promise of fruit harvest; but some poor hungry Cockney in another generation,' he adds, 'may do better'.

The garden lay to the east of the house. From the back door, three steps led down to a yard or 'back area', paved with flagstones, from which one step led up to a gravel path, bordered with box. The path branched to the left between flower beds, and led to the earth closet, a square brick building almost hidden in summer by lilac bushes and fruit-trees. Beyond the second flower bed the path again turned to the left, and then ran eastwards alongside a narrow border where the vines grew against the wall. On the other side of the path was a rough oblong patch of grass; another flower bed ran between the grass and the north wall; and the path led round the top of the garden, past the ashpit, to the south-east corner. Here, in February 1860, Nero was buried under a little stone tablet commemorating the date of his death.

Jane was to complain, in 1843, that Carlyle never dreamt of lying in the shade of his own walnut-tree—'it is a tree! leaves as green as any leaves can be!'—and must needs go as far afield as Wales for rest and refreshment. But for the most part it was Thomas, not Jane, who walked and sat in the garden. 'It was,' he said, 'of admirable comfort . . . in the *smoking* way,' and to the end of his life he wandered and smoked there, keeping short clay pipes tucked away in niches of the old walls, filled and ready for use. In the small hours he would sometimes go out into the garden when sleep deserted him, to smoke and meditate under the stars.

'Sunday I started broad awake at 3 a.m., went downstairs, out, smoked a cigar on a stool; have not seen so lovely, sad, and grand a summer weather scene for twenty years back', he wrote in August 1857. 'Trees stood all as if cast in bronze, not an aspen leaf stirring; sky was a silver mirror, getting yellowish to the north-east; and only one big star, star of the morning, visible in the increasing light.'

That same hot summer two curious Chinese seats, 'little china barrel-shaped things', green in colour, made their appearance. There is a photograph of Carlyle sitting on one, but they must have been very cold and hard, and it is not surprising to find him referring to them as ornaments. Jane, he said, was 'busy ornamenting the garden', these green china stools being part of her scheme. Some years earlier a low brick parapet had been built, dividing the yard from the rest of the garden, with low square pediments at each end and on either side of the step, where she stood pots of flowers, probably the hardy London geranium.

That summer of 1857 Jane decided to make an awning, so that Carlyle might work out of doors, shaded from the 'blazes of July'. It may be remembered that during the earthquake of 1843 Jane took refuge in a home-made tent in the garden, where—in spite of the curious heads peering out at her 'from all the windows of *the Row*'— she was able to write and sew in peace. She now planned something more elaborate, and less liable to be blown down by a gust of wind.

It consisted of sheets, sewn together and tied at one end to a pole which was attached at right-angles to the garden wall; the loose sides were strung at intervals to the branches of trees. The sultry weather duly arrived, the awning went up, and Carlyle carried out a small table and a kitchen chair, and worked under its shade; and Jane went off to Scotland feeling that her invention was a success.

The indefatigable Robert Tait ('that weary Artist who took the bright idea last spring that he would make a Picture of our sitting-room—to be "amazingly interesting to Posterity a hundred years hence" ') carried his photographic apparatus upstairs to a second-floor window and produced several pictures of Carlyle under the awning. Jane had had enough of Tait and his photography. He had not yet started his famous painting, but was busily taking preliminary portraits of Carlyle, of Jane, even of Nero, with his camera. 'Tait gives me the idea of a man going mad rather than gathering sense', she now wrote. 'The little figures under the awning* however *are* charming; and one won't grudge him a little "fame" for these "a hundred years hence".'

The hot weather broke. Carlyle, with no Jane to drive him indoors, went on correcting proofs under the awning. After a day or two he began to feel feverish and headachy, 'which I at first attributed to oxtail soup, but now discover to be cold caught sitting in the sweep of the wind'.

Nevertheless, Jane's invention must have been a success, for seven years later, in the summer of 1863, the awning, or something like it, was still being used, nearer the house. 'Mr. Carlyle has got his tent up in the back area', Jane wrote on 5 July, 'and writes away there without much inconvenience, as yet, from the heat.'

Summers in Chelsea were often oppressively hot, and the Carlyles, bred in colder, stronger air, felt the need to get away. There were dreams of a cottage by the sea—at Aldeburgh—at Rottingdean, 'an old sleepy-looking little village' to which Jane had walked from Brighton. On her way back she lay on the cliffs: 'Oh, what beautiful sea!' she cried, 'blue as the Firth of Forth it was last night!' But after her day at Brighton she returned to Cheyne Row; the dreams faded with the passing of summer, and Chelsea remained Jane's only home, to be made the best of: the banks of the Thames her substitute for the sea-shore; and the Cheyne Row garden, 'so called in the language of flattery', her only equivalent for the fertile country-side of her youth.

There was little sentimentality in Jane's nature, but what there was expressed itself in her garden. She tried to fill it with flowers that reminded her of Scotland and of the places and people she loved. In the summer of 1836 she brought back two roots of heather from Templand, hoping to see them 'in brisk action at Cheyne Row'; and—undaunted by disappointments—she never returned from Scotland without a bundle of plants. She brought roses from Templand, and after her mother's death Mary Russell sent her slips and

*Carlyle and Nero.

cuttings from plants which Mrs. Welsh had grown—polyanthus, jessamine, sweetbrier. The Templand sweetbrier did not take to London soil. It prospered well at first, 'too well, I suppose', wrote Jane, 'for it hurried itself to put out leaves when it should have been quietly taking root—a procedure not confined to sweetbriers; one sees many human beings go off in the same fashion'. The devoted Mary sent another slip, which was killed by heavy rains in 1852. Jane was upset, and admitted that she could not help feeling 'the sweetbrier's unwillingness to grow with me a bad omen somehow'. 'I wonder,' she asked Mrs. Russell, 'if you will be good-natured and unwearied enough to send me another slip when the right time comes?'

This sweetbrier must also have been unwilling, for five years later, in November 1857, we find Jane again writing to Mary Russell, 'Every letter I have forgotten to speak of the sweetbrier—I should like *you* to keep it over the Winter, and send it in the Spring.—It will surely grow with me then.'

'A good joy,' said Leigh Hunt's child at the sight of flowers; and Jane echoed this sentiment. 'Ask for a bouquet for me,' she begged Carlyle, returning from a visit to the Ashburtons. His voluntary factotum, Mr. Larkin, often brought posies for Jane from his London garden, and invited her, in the summer of 1858, to spend the day with his mother 'in that beautiful garden from which he brings me such bouquets'. Erasmus Darwin came to see her bringing 'three beautiful hyacinths in pots—a white, a blue and a pink'. And on a 'cold, rasping savage day' in March 1856, when the east wind 'blew knives and files', she was cheered immeasurably by a bunch of violets and a bouquet of 'the loveliest most fragrant flowers' given her by Geraldine Jewsbury—'as if she would contend with the elements on my behalf'.

But it was Scottish flowers that pleased her best: even the thought of them gave her pleasure. 'Have you any snowdrops or crocuses in bloom?' she asks Mary Russell at the end of a mild winter. A few snowdrops enclosed in a letter from her cousin Walter Welsh of Auchtertool delighted her. 'They arrived as *flat* as could be; but when I put them in water, I could positively see them

drinking and their little bellies rounding themselves out, till they
looked as fresh as if they had just been brought in from the garden.'
And when at last she brought herself to revisit Haddington, seven
years after her mother's death, 'Everybody is so good to me, so very
good!' she exclaimed when a bouquet 'out of your own garden'
was presented to her by one of the family now living in her old
home.

When she returned to London she brought with her a nettle,
uprooted from Mrs. Welsh's grave in Crawford church-yard, and a
'little thing with two tiny leaves' which she found growing on her
father's grave in Haddington. These were duly planted in the
garden and tended with loving care; and in time the 'little green
thing' proved to be a gooseberry plant. 'Oh! be kind to Nero, and
slightly attentive to the canaries, and my poor little nettle and
gooseberry bush,' she begged Carlyle, eight years later. The
previous autumn she had brought home plants (as well as canaries)
from Scotland; and endured the familiar misery of watching the life
slowly deserting them and the leaves beginning to droop. 'My poor
little plants,' she cried, 'don't know whether to live or die.'

But the nettle and the gooseberry, being wild things, flourished.
Year after year they went on, neglected and unnoticed during Jane's
illness when Carlyle, immersed in 'Frederick', left the garden to
look after itself. In the end, a gardener was found, an old man whom
Jane called 'little darling'. He was, said Carlyle, a careful and good
gardener; but in September 1860, he came to Jane with his arm in a
sling: it was paralysed. He 'repeatedly broke down into tears,' said
Jane, 'and made me cry too. "Oh!" he said, "how I do miss my poor
dear—" I thought he was going to say wife . . . but no, it was
"arm"! "Oh, how I miss my poor dear arm!" He didn't need money,
wouldn't even be paid what was owing him. . . .'

It seems unlikely that 'little darling' was able to work in the
garden again, and by 1863 he was succeeded by another old man for
whom Jane had no affection. He made short work of her nettle,
which he could not believe to be anything but a weed. When she
asked him if the gooseberry bush could be got to bear 'if it were only
*one* gooseberry', he held out no hopes. ' "A poor wild thing. No; if

you want to have gooseberries, ma'am, better get a proper gooseberry bush in its place." ' Jane was outraged.

'The old Goth!' she cried. 'He can't be made to understand that
things can have any value but just their garden value.' And she went
on to describe how, 'in spite of all I could beg and direct', he had
rooted out her nettle. What could a Cockney gardener know of the
complexity of feeling that had inspired the preservation of those
two Scottish weeds?

That summer, the gooseberry bush, as if in defiance of the Old
Goth, produced three gooseberries. 'I rushed out, excited as a child,
to look at them,' said Jane. 'But alas!' she continues, 'whether it was
through too much staring at them, or too much east wind, or
through mere delicacy in the "poor wild thing", I can't tell; only the
result, that the three bits of gooseberries, instead of growing larger,
grew every day less, till they reached the smallness of pin-heads,
and then dropped on the ground! I could have cried when they
went.'

The gooseberry bush outlived Jane, and lived to bear a crop of
fruit. 'It still stands there, green and leafy, and with berries', wrote
Carlyle after her death; 'how strange and memorable to me now!'

To replace the nettle, on her next visit to Scotland she dug up
another root from her mother's grave, which she brought home in a
pot and 'emptied without shaking into our garden'. She brought as
well some 'Strathmilligan woodruff', a daisy from Templand, and a
piece of ivy which took to the London soil and rampaged all over
the end of the south wall. The sweetbrier had failed her, and some
of the more delicate plants; but many of her Scottish flowers lingered
after her death, reminders now, not of Jane's nostalgia for Scotland,
but of Jane; and Carlyle wandered up and down the garden mourn-
fully considering 'HER little gooseberry bush (brought hither
from her Father's Grave . . .): her Hawthorn, Ash-tree, etc., all
from loved scenes of childhood. . . .'

In February 1868, nearly two years after her death, her plants
were once again 'in vigorous bud, almost in leaf'. 'This is the
brightest February, for weather, I ever saw,' Carlyle wrote in his
journal; 'nor are its sad remembrances without some use to me. . . .'

The garden continued to be kept neat and free from weeds; the gravel paths were rolled and the grass cut; the vine was pruned, and produced year after year its two or three bunches of small sweet grapes. Mr. Carlyle's fat tabby cat crouched in the undergrowth as its predecessors had done, watching the birds; and in the summer lay on the warm flags; and Carlyle, seeing it beside his chair, would remember how Nero had lain there in the old days, jumping up to remind him when it was dinner time.

A virginia creeper was planted in the 1870's, against the north wall; Mrs. Allingham sketched the old man sitting beside it, in his hat and long overcoat, with his cat in attendance and his church-warden pipe laid on the grass, ready for use. The garden was still, at the end of his life, 'of admirable comfort . . . in the *smoking* way,' and innumerable small pieces of his pipe-stems made their way into the thin soil, slowly burying themselves among the roots or being pushed to the surface again by the shifting earth.

CHAPTER ELEVEN

## 'A Most Fearful Item'

'**M**Y goodness,' cried Jane, 'why make bits of apologies for writing about the servants—as if "the *servants*" were not a most important—a most fearful item in our female existence!'

Here without a 'bit of apology' then is yet another chapter concerning this fearful item, whose humours and problems occupied a considerable part of the domestic life at Cheyne Row.

After the end of Helen's long and chequered career there was a period during which no servant was able, for more than a few months at best, to keep Jane's good opinion. We hear of sulks and bad temper, of dishonesty and incompetence; and at one point in 1851, the servants come and go with such rapidity that even their names are not mentioned, and it is difficult to discover who is out and who in.

There was much interviewing of prospective servants, of which Jane has left us two classic examples. The first was a refined young woman with a three years' character and a talent for cooking fish ('all sorts of fish in all sorts of ways'. 'Pity we never eat fish,' said Jane). 'I remarked that she did not look very strong—the answer was "perhaps I look more delicate for being in mourning— mourning . . . is *such a denial* to a young person".'

This delicate flower quickly vanished from the scene—in fact, we never hear of her again—and it is to be hoped that she found a place where her talent for cooking fish was appreciated.

A woman 'with a face to split a pitcher' would have been hard put to it to gain Jane's good opinion, even if she had gone about things the right way. But this one 'came seemingly to hire *me*', wrote Jane. 'After surveying me—rather contemptuously I must own—she proceeded to ask me a string of questions, which I answered to see how it would end. "Did I keep no more servants than *one*?" "Had I much company?" "Was I in the habit of often changing my servants?" ' This was a challenge—but Jane met it. 'I answered as often as they seemed to require changing, and on the whole I *shouldn't suit her*, I was afraid.'

From 1852 the household settled down again: there were six years of Ann—'a thoroughly good, respectable woman—the best character I ever had'—'punctual, trustworthy, I hope she will stay for ever'. . . . This was Ann II, whose name Jane *usually* spells without the final e: 'hard, practical Ann', who demanded £16 a year and a regular meat dinner at one o'clock. But this was also the Ann who had to be rushed to the Apothecary with a beetle in her ear, an incident which for the time being broke down her usual calm. She was a steady, superior servant, cared well, said Jane, for Mr. C.'s material comforts, and when she cut her finger chopping up a bath- brick, told Lady Alice Hill, 'I did it in cutting up a fowl!' 'You know, ma'am,' she explained to Jane, 'I couldn't go and say to a *real* young Lady that I did it cutting a bath-brick—that sounded so *common!*'

But by February 1858 she was 'that unblessed Anne', 'cunning, untrue, and intensely selfish', and when she gave notice it was a relief. Ann intended, she said, to find 'a situation with a single gentleman who kept an under servant to do all the rough work'. 'Don't she wish she may get it?' said Jane.

But in comparison with her successor, Ann must have seemed a pearl. For Jane now tried a bold experiment.

'It is in the nature of an adventure,' she wrote to Mary Russell, 'my last choice of a servant! How it will turn out, heaven only knows. Oh, my dear, only fancy! I have hired a "Miss Cameron" (from Inverness), "daughter of a half-pay lieutenant". . . .' Miss Cameron, with her intelligent affectionate face and modest but self-possessed manner, confessed disarmingly that she had no idea whether she could clean a house or cook a dinner, but hoped that she would soon learn. She did not have time, for after seventeen days she was 'convicted of lying and theft', and ran out of the house at night, never to be seen again.

Carlyle was furious.

'My poor little sick partner,' he exclaimed, 'I declare it is heartbreaking for her sake, *disgusting* otherwise to a high degree, and *dirtier* for the mind than even brushing of boots oneself would be for the body.'

Fortunately by this time Jane had found a Chelsea woman, Mrs. Newnham, who was 'an astonishingly good cook', and who would always come in during a crisis and see to the meals. 'The cares of bread' as Jane called them, quoting Mazzini, were thus temporarily relieved. Carlyle was becoming more and more difficult to feed, so that from now on it became of paramount importance to find a servant who could cook.

But this time, worn out by scenes, and perhaps remembering the comparative peacefulness of her dealings with 'little girls'—with Sereetha the Peesweep, Eliza, and little Martha, who obliged when Ann was ill—Jane engaged another child and decided to train her. Charlotte Southam was 15—'a fine little Chelsea creature,' said Carlyle—and she lived with her aunt and uncle (whom she called mother and father) just round the corner in Lawrence Street. She had a round, rosy face; she was merry and anxious to please; Jane took to her instantly.

'Charlotte is as kind and attentive as possible', she wrote to Carlyle who had gone to Scotland, 'and her speech is remarkably sensible. She was observing yesterday morning that "Master" looked rather dull at going away; "and I can't say," she added, "that you look particularly brilliant (!) since his departure".'

This was discerning of Charlotte. 'Master' was in the depths of gloom when he left, with a dinner packed up by Jane to eat on the long train journey. 'I was', he wrote, 'discontented with myself, with hot fetid London, generally with all persons and things—and my stomach had struck work withal. But not discontented', he assured her, 'with poor you ever at all.' (Jane had suggested bitterly, 'I have neither the strength and spirits to bear up against your discontent, nor the obtuseness to be indifferent to it . . . in fact . . . the only feasible and dignified thing that remains for one to do is just to die, and be done with it!')

Alone with Charlotte, Jane cheered up. She was delighted with her new protégé. 'My young maid is a jewel of a creature,' she wrote, 'much kinder and helpfuller than Anne was . . . a good, biddable, clever little creature.' She took advantage of Carlyle's absence to teach Charlotte how to cook meals to suit him: to make the clear essence of beef of which he took a breakfast-cupful 'almost daily'; to broil his chops and bake his milk puddings and home-made bread; to give him plenty of old potatoes, well boiled, and no other vegetable; to make his nightly bowl of porridge or broad-berry ('Master's pap,' Ann called it)—and to brew his morning coffee.

She explained how the shopping was done. Jane herself bought the tea and coffee from Fortnum and Mason; potatoes and oatmeal came from Scotland, but groceries and meat, butter and eggs, came from local shops. The milkman was Mr. Shakespear, but the cream had to be got from Mr. Wright's cows—and poor stuff it was com-pared with the beautiful yellow cream from Lord Ashburton's farm at Addiscombe. At Christmas time one of Mr. Carlyle's sisters generally sent a hamper packed with good country fare—a goose, chickens, new-laid eggs. Local eggs, said Jane, were unreliable. Mr. Carlyle did not always notice if you gave him a shop egg for his breakfast, but if one happened to be 'too far gone for his making an illusion about it' there was an explosion.

Mr. Carlyle liked to dine late—at seven or even eight—and after dinner he had to be restrained from drinking innumerable cups of tea, which kept him awake. Jane preferred to take her dinner at two. She enjoyed roasted larks, sweetbreads—more dainty and adventurous meals than her husband; she enjoyed strawberries and cream, seldom touched other fruit; but she was not averse to fresh vegetables, when they were to be had.

One day Jane 'took a notion of' mince collops for dinner, and taught Charlotte how to make them. The meat, she said, should be chopped very small. 'Don't you think, Ma'am,' said Charlotte, 'if I *scraped* it,—and made it for you as I used to do for my blackbird, it would be better than chopping?'

Charlotte's experience of feeding a blackbird must have stood her in good stead when, a week or two after her arrival, Jane rescued a sparrow from some streetboys and brought it home. It could not feed itself. 'I have to put crowdy into its mouth (which is always gaping) with a stick,' said Jane.

At the end of July, Charlotte was put in charge, not only of the sparrow, but of the house: Jane had decided to go away. This time Nero stayed at Cheyne Row; Mr. Piper the postman agreed to take him out on his rounds, and Charlotte was ready to take care of him, as well as getting on with the chimney-sweeping and 'thoroughcleaning'. 'Charlotte is more to be trusted with the house,' she assured Carlyle, 'than Ann was; she has quite as much sense and infinitely more principle. . . . Her Mother will come and sleep with her.'

Charlotte was an unqualified success; Jane could see no fault in her. She was already, said her mistress, a better cook than Ann. She was also a *very* good housemaid; moreover, she did what she was told, at the first word: 'she is my *servant*—and not my Mistress!'

Jane's first letter home, written on 5 August, shows that already there was a bond between mistress and maid; and it is evident that Charlotte had begun to appreciate Jane's jokes.

'Oh, little woman! little woman!' wrote Jane, 'I wonder how you get on there, all by yourself, in 'that highly *genteel* seven-roomed House" (as the retired cheesemonger would describe it). If you hadn't made ducks and drakes of your opportunities; and preferred sitting drearily at the upstairs window looking out into the street; you might by this time have been up to writing me a nice little letter; to your own honour and glory! as well as to *my* peace of mind; seeing that I can't help making myself anxious about you; when day after day passes, and I hear nothing from home—not a word either from you, or the dog, or the sparrow!'

In spite of her anxiety, she was very much better, she told Charlotte, and had made up her mind to stay on and enjoy the sea air for another week. Mr. Larkin, she said, would bring Charlotte another 6*s*. for her keep; and she must find some fresh work to keep her occupied, 'that you mayn't, in my absence, scrape acquaintance with a certain person, who, I told you, was "always at the elbow of an idle girl!"—And that I may see cause to commend your diligence when I return!

'Tell Nero, with my dear love, that I fervently hope he is not overeating himself! And to the Sparrow give, in my name, a good-sized worm!

'God keep you a good girl!' she ends, and signs herself, 'Yours kindly.'

Charlotte lost no time in sending a reassuring and extremely self-possessed reply.

'Dear Madam,—I have taken the liberty of answering your kind letter, thinking you would like to know that the house is quite safe, and that me and Nero are quite well and happy, he is very good company for me, the sparrow is doing very well, and Dear Madam I will do my best to keep that Certen person at a distance from my elbow.

'. . . I am happy to hear that you are better and that the air agrees with you so well.

'So no more from you Obedient servant,

CHARLOTTE SOUTHAM.'

Jane was delighted with this effort which showed, she said 'both consideration and energy'. 'But the penmanship', she exclaimed, 'was never your own surely! It would have been too much modesty to tell me you "could not write" if you were up to writing like *that*! It might very soon be made into an excellent hand, that! and I shall feel it more than ever incumbent on me to make you write a little every evening instead of looking out at the upstairs window!'

She again postponed her homecoming, but took the precaution of ordering her dinner in advance, 'that you mayn't be troubling your youthful brain with uncertainties as to *what* I would like'. She would like, she said, minced mutton browned before the fire, and a ground rice pudding—'and you must please give me *enough*!!' The sea air had improved her appetite.

She came home to find that the sparrow had died; otherwise everything was serene, and as soon as she had freshened up her clothes—her bonnet ribbons were 'frightfully dirty' and her white shawl 'ditto'—she set off for Scotland. Charlotte and Nero went to Euston Square to see her off; and soon Jane was writing long letters to her little maid from Lann Hall in Dumfries, in which directions about house-cleaning and admonitions to further industry were mixed with news of her own doings. She was impressed, she told Charlotte, by her hostess's 'talent for housekeeping'. 'We must improve, you and I', she added.

This was the first hint of criticism—of herself as well as Charlotte. Perhaps she had been too indulgent, too easily pleased. She proceeded to issue a few orders. 'You must get on with your house-sorting, . . . It will be a great shame to you, if you have not the house perfectly sorted when we return—having for so long had no family to attend to but Nero. In particular, I wish you would give the drawing-room grate not one but several good scourings,' she goes on; 'I did not at all admire the state in which you were letting it lie over till wanted!'

'When you clean the furniture,' went on Jane firmly, 'ask Mrs. Newnham to mix you some beeswax and soap, as *she* knows how—and then use it *very sparingly* indeed, having first *carefully washed the furniture with soap and warmish water*.' 'You should rub up the four-posted beds', she went on, 'as well as the dining room chairs, &c. . . .'

There was little chance for Charlotte to lapse into idleness. John

Carlyle was expected to turn up at any moment and was to have the run of the house—but 'Don't bring out any china or little things,' wrote Jane, 'Dr. Carlyle is dangerous for *breaking*.' The carpets had to be re-laid and curtains re-hung; and a mattress ticking collected from the cleaners and stuffed.

But Jane found it necessary to apply a spur.

'If you saw how all things *do shine* in this house! and yet I should say by the look of her face that the housemaid here is neither so active nor so clever a girl as you are. . . .'

On 16 September she moved from Lann Hall to stay with the Russells at Thornhill, and learnt that Carlyle (who was in Germany) had decided to return straight to Chelsea instead of joining her in Scotland as she had expected. She was worried.

'I must just trust to your making him comfortable for a week or two', she wrote to Charlotte. 'You know his ways and what he needs pretty well by this time . . . If you take pains to please him I have no doubt you will.' But as she wrote she grew more anxious, thinking of Carlyle after long journeys and strange beds, bilious and exhausted. 'If he look fussed and *cross*,' she proceeded, 'never mind, so long as you are doing your best; travelling always puts him in a fever, and nobody can look and speak amiably with sick nerves.' And of course he might easily change his plans again.

'You need not order in anything till Mr. C. arrive—or till he tell you he is positively coming—then get what is needed at your own discretion, without troubling *him*.'

Her faith in Charlotte's good sense was remarkable; but she added,

'Heaven help you and him well thro' it!'

Once she knew Carlyle was back, Jane could not rest: a week later she returned home, with a hamper of food from The Gill ('not so much as one egg was broken! And such satisfaction was diffused over the house by the unpacking', she wrote) and a skep of honey from Thornhill. To her relief, everything was 'extremely right' at Cheyne Row. 'Indeed, I never found (my house) as thoroughly cleaned, or the general aspect of things as satisfactory. She is a perfect jewel, that young girl; besides all her natural work, she had crocheted, out of her own head, a large cover for the drawing-room sofa!'

After the impassive, undemonstrative Ann, it was a joy to be greeted by Charlotte's dancing spirits and face radiant with good humour and kindliness. If Charlotte had ever fallen in her esteem, she was now reinstated.

'I find all extremely right here,' Jane told Mary Russell. 'A perfectly cleaned house, and a little maid radiant with "virtue its own reward".'

'I think Scotland must be such a fresh, airy place!' Charlotte said next day. 'I should like to go there. You did smell so beautiful when you came in at the door last night.'

The following year, Charlotte did go to Scotland. Jane had been miserably ill, and in the summer of 1859 Carlyle rented 'the tolerable upper floor' of a farm-house at Humbie in Fifeshire. Charlotte travelled all the way by boat with her master, her master's horse Fritz, and Nero; while Jane, on her doctor's advice, made her own way by train.

For Charlotte this holiday was an unforgettable adventure.

The farm-house, said Jane, looked out on 'the beautifullest view in the world', and there was 'an abundance of what Mr. C. calls "soft food" (new milk, fresh eggs, whey, &c.).' Charlotte, she said, was the happiest of girls. 'Not that she seems to have much sensibility for the "Beauties of Nature" . . . but that the "kindness of Scotch people" fills her with wonder and delight. "Young men that don't so much as know her name, passing her on the road, say to her, "Bonnie wee lassie!" And the farmer here gave her "a little sugar rabbit" and said to her "Little girl, you are growing quite pretty since you came".'

The holiday lasted for two months, and even Jane felt some benefit. 'We hear dreadful accounts of the heat in London and the smell of the river!' she wrote to Charlotte's aunt, Mrs. Southam, who was looking after the house. 'We are lucky to be here, I think, where it is quite cool and nothing smelling but roses.'

That autumn, in recognition of his work on *Frederick the Great*, Carlyle received from Germany the Order of the White Falcon.

'Charlotte told our charwoman with great glee, that the Master might call himself "Sir Thomas, if he liked"', Jane wrote to Mrs. Russell. ' "My!" said the charwoman, "then the Mistress is Lady, now!" "Yes," said Charlotte, "but she says she won't go in for it! Such a shame!" '

Charlotte was established, a member of the household: 'far more like an adopted child than a London maid-of-all-work', said Jane, and gave her a pinchbeck brooch containing a portrait of Nero; a sewing-case, a photograph of herself, and a lock of hair. 'The strange little being,' she said, 'has so much good sense and reflection in her, that she is quite as good to talk with as most of the fine ladies that come about me.'

It was impossible that such a state of affairs could last.

Perhaps the holiday in Scotland was demoralizing, and the little cockney sparrow never settled down properly to her work after the excitement of seeing so many new places and people, and hearing herself called 'a bonnie wee lassie' by strange kind Scots. Jane's letters to her from The Grange, in January 1860, are as affectionate and confiding as ever, but there is a hint that Charlotte's industry is not what it was. Mr. C., she says, has been ill and cross, and may return home suddenly at any moment: Charlotte must take care to be ready for him, 'that if he do start off all on a sudden, he mayn't be put in a rage at the end of his journey by finding nobody to get him some dinner, or what he needs'.

'As for the cleaning,' she goes on, 'don't have more than *one* thing in hands at any time—and then you can't be found in any *irremediable* muddle come when we may!'

Muddle was Charlotte's downfall. She evidently needed Jane's constant nagging to keep up with her work; she was sluggish and inclined to oversleep; when her mistress was ill, things went from bad to worse. The *dénouement* has not been recorded, but in the summer of 1860 Charlotte was dismissed. There must have been a scene, for Jane was soon to repent of her haste. Charlotte, she said, excusing herself, needed 'to be put under some *stricter* superintendence than mine'.

Now—going from one extreme to the other—she engaged an 'old

Treasure' of 71; who stipulated that on the Master's return from Scotland she must be supplied with 'a pair of young legs' to assist her.

The 'pair of young legs' arrived, a girl of 16 called Sarah: but already the aged Treasure had beaten a hasty retreat, carrying off eight bottles of ale with her. 'An arrant old humbug!' cried Jane— 'a perfectly incompetent cook and servant.'

Now somebody had to be found 'to be head to the girl'. 'I was weak enough,' said Jane 'to wish to take Charlotte back, but not weak enough to *do it*! *She*, who couldn't rule *herself*, would have made a sad mess of ruling a girl nearly her own age. So I had to engage a middle-aged servant. . . .'

This was Charlotte II—known as Tall Charlotte: she was, said Jane, who by now had influenza, 'a good nurse, very quiet and kindly, and with sense to do things without being told. I have not had my clothes folded neatly up, and the room tidied, and my wants anticipated in this way since I had no longer any mother to nurse me.'

'I am glad,' she added, 'that I had the strength to resist (Charlotte's) tears and her request to be taken back as cook. I told her some day I might take her back, but she had much to learn and unlearn first. Still, it is gratifying to feel that one's kindness to the girl has not been all lost on her, for she really loves both of us passionately. . . .'

Carlyle came home from Scotland at the end of September; in Jane's view he had not benefited from his long holiday so much as she had hoped. 'He still goes on waking up several times in the night—when he bolts up, and smokes, and sometimes takes a cold bath!' Jane, lying sleepless waiting for the sound of Carlyle jumping out of bed in the room above, began to long for the kindly affection and sympathy of little Charlotte. Nowadays, she could not even set foot in her own kitchen without black looks. By the end of October she was ready, as she put it, to hang herself.

'With *one* servant—especially with one *Charlotte*,' she wrote to Mary Russell, 'we were *one* family in the House; one interest and *one* Power! Now it is as if I had taken in *Lodgers* for downstairs; and had a flight of crows about me for upstairs! I ring my bell, this one answers, but it is "the other's business" to do what I want. Then the solemn consultations about "*your* dinner" and "*our* dinner', the everlasting smell of fresh turpentine, without anything looking cleaner than it used to be; the ever-recurring "we", which in little Charlotte's mouth meant Master and Mistress and self; but in the mouth of the new tall Charlotte means—most decidedly "I and Sarah".'

'Shall I ever get used to it?' she cried, and she wrote to Mrs. Austin, 'Often in the dead of night I am seized with a wild desire to clear the house of these new-comers, and take back my one little Charlotte, who is still hanging on at her mother's, in a wild hope that one or other of them, or both, may break down, and she be reinstated in her place.'

Charlotte could not keep away.

'What a fool that girl is,' tall Charlotte said to Jane. 'I told her she should look out for a place, that a nice looking healthy girl like her might easily find one; and she answered, "Oh, yes! I may get plenty of places, but never a *home* again, as I have had here".'

'Tall Charlotte,' said Jane, 'could only see folly in such attachment. "She is very different from I am," said she; "if people hadn't been satisfied with *me*, it's little I should care about leaving them." . . . "I can well believe that," said I, with a strong disposition to knock her down.'

A month later little Charlotte was back, and her tall namesake, now referred to as 'that vulgar, conceited woman' was gone for good. 'Upon my word,' wrote Jane, 'I haven't been as near what they call "happy" for many a day.'

As for Charlotte, said Jane, she was 'so bursting with ecstasy as she ran up and down the house, taking possession, as it were, of her old work, . . . that it was impossible not to share her delighted excitement!' She was engaged as cook, but she insisted upon opening the door to visitors, 'to show herself, and receive their congratulations'.

The two young girls, Charlotte and Sarah, were a good combination. 'Sarah's tidiness and method are just what were wanted to correct little Charlotte's born tendency to muddle; while little

Charlotte's willingness and affectionateness warm up Sarah's drier, more selfish nature.'

'It is a curious establishment,' Jane added, 'with something of the sound and character of a nursery. Charlotte not nineteen till next March, and Sarah seventeen last week, and they keep up an incessant chirping and chattering and laughing; and as both have remarkably sweet voices, it is pleasant to hear.'

They slept in the basement kitchen. As neither could wake up in the morning, an old man who lodged with Charlotte's aunt in Lawrence Street was asked to bang on the window with his stick as he passed on his way to work. An hour later Charlotte's uncle would rap again.

Jane also supplied them with an alarm clock.

'It runs down at six,' she said, 'at their very bed-head, and is never heard by either of these fortunate girls.'

This happy situation was too good to last. In the summer Charlotte gave notice: she wished, she explained 'to better herself'. This was a turning of the tables indeed, and Jane was deeply hurt: Charlotte had 'taken up with people and things unworthy of her'. 'Oh, child! child! you have no idea of the disappointment, the heartsorrow you caused me! I had set so much love on you, and so much hope! So much permanent good was to come out of our chance-relation for both of us! And all ending in a mere vulgar commonplace disruption betwixt *Mistress* and *Maid*!'

Charlotte had taken a place as an under-housemaid in a big country house near Sevenoaks. Jane was bitterly disappointed in her 'adopted daughter'. After all her 'aspirations after knowledge and refinement', all she looked for were higher wages and a bigger establishment. For more than a year there was silence between them.

Then, in March 1863, Charlotte sent her former mistress a box of violets. Jane was touched. 'It was a nice thought,' she wrote, 'A kind little practical thought!—just like my little Charlotte in her *good* Time—before she had become stubborn and callous on my hands. . . .'

'Do you know,' she went on, 'the violets found me breakfasting in bed . . . and their sweet smell reminded me somehow of your kind nursing in my long Influenza. No one has nursed me as kindly and as cleverly since!'

The breach was healed. A few weeks later Charlotte knocked at the door of number 5.

'You remember my little Charlotte?' Jane wrote to Betty Braid, 'I had a visit from her yesterday, and she looks much more sedate and proper than when I had to put her away. She is "third house-maid at the Marquis of Camden's", and lives in the country, which is good for her.'

Charlotte was one of the few people to whom Jane sent an account of her street accident in St. Martin's-le-Grand.

'For days and nights I lay unable to move, in dreadful agony, and without a wink of sleep,' she told her. 'My maids have been most kind and attentive to me,' she added; but in her weakness and pain, Jane must have longed for the affectionate concern of little Charlotte, the only servant, apart from the ill-starred Helen, who had made Cheyne Row her home.

'No servant has ever been for me the sort of adopted child that you were.'

Meanwhile, Jane 'puddled on' with Mrs. Newnham coming in to cook, and a new housemaid called Margaret—Welsh, said Jane—Irish, said Carlyle: 'a little black busy creature, who did very well for some time; but, &c. &c. (some mysterious love-affair, I think)—and went to New Zealand out of sight'.

Etcetera, etcetera . . . so each brief history was to end. By now, Jane was often too invalidish to enter into the battle with the same zest: but from time to time there are echoes of the old dramas, comic or tragic—and once again, as if in a flash of lighting, another character stands out vividly for a few moments, only to disappear for ever into obscurity.

Elizabeth came from East Lothian in May 1862—'as harmless a piece of human nature as was ever put into my hands to work up into a "good plain cook"'. 'Oh, so *very* plain it must be,' sighed Jane. By November Elizabeth was 'my Scotch blockhead'. 'Mr. C.,' said his wife, 'always speaks of her as "that horse", "that cow", "that

mooncalf".' She earned these epithets by her extraordinary talent
for breakages. She broke the glass of the back door 'three several
times . . . three times, in the six months she has been here! and
nobody before ever smashed that door!' She was ingenious and
wholesale in her demolition, contriving somehow to upset the
kitchen table, a solid deal affair planted firmly on its square legs,
'and smash at one stroke nearly all the tumblers and glasses . . .
all the china breakfast things, a crystal butter-glass . . . a crystal
flower vase, and ever so many jugs and bowls! There was a whole
washing-tub full of broken things!' 'Surely honesty, sobriety, and
steadiness must have grown dreadfully scarce qualities,' said Jane
wearily, 'that one puts up with such a cook; especially as her cooking
is as careless as the rest of her doings. . . . Every third day,' she
continues, a meal is set before Mr. C. 'that provokes him into
declaring "That brute will be the death of me!"'

It is not surprising to find that within another week Elizabeth
was packing her box and going back to East Lothian, and Jane was
running up and down the basement stairs 'teaching breadmaking,
and Mr. C.'s sort of soup, and Mr. C.'s sort of puddings, cutlets, &c.
&c.,' all over again. But a year later she was still looking back 'with
a shudder over the six months of that East Lothian Elizabeth! Her
dinners blackened to cinders! her constant crashes of glass and
china! her brutal manners! her lumpish insensibility and in-
gratitude!' 'And to think,' she went on 'that that woman must
have been considered above the average of East Lothian servants.
What an idea it gives one of the state of things in East Lothian!'
But in time Jane was to realize that there was another, more sinister
side to the story, of which she was as yet unconscious.

Meanwhile, there had been trouble with housemaids. Margaret
was succeeded by Maria, a refined and an emotional young woman
who danced round Jane, covering her hands and shawl with kisses.
'I should have lost patience with her long ago, if it hadn't been for
her cleverness about Mr. C.'s books, which I fancied would make
him extremely averse to parting with her.' Carlyle worked in the
attic, but many of his books were kept in the drawing-room, two
floors below; it saved him trouble if he could ring and have books

brought up to him, but as Jane said, cleverness in finding what he needed was 'not a common gift with housemaids'. Maria was riding for a fall, however, when—fancying herself indispensable to her master—she began to put on airs, was impertinent to Jane, 'picking and choosing at her work—in fact, not behaving like a servant at all, but like a lady, who, for a caprice, or a wager, or anything except wages and board, was condescending to exercise light functions in the house, provided you kept her in good humour with gifts and praises'.

Jane was not one to endure such a state of affairs for long; and to her relief 'when Mr. C.'s attention was directed to her procedure, he saw the intolerableness as clearly as I did'. The Sage's verdict was harsh: Maria was 'an affected fool' and had better 'carry her fantasticalities and incompetences elsewhere'.

Maria was followed by 'little Flo'—'not a little dog, as you might fancy from the name, but a remarkably intelligent, well-conditioned girl between fourteen and fifteen, who was christened "Florence"—too long and too romantic a name', Jane considered, 'for household use'.

Fortunately Flo's cleverness so impressed Carlyle that he was 'much less aggravating than usual under a change'. 'Training her,' said Jane, 'is next to no trouble.' But she was determined not to praise and pet her overmuch, and so, spoil her, as she had spoilt Charlotte. There was little temptation, however; Flo lacked Charlotte's charm—there was 'something dry and hard, something very *unyouthful* in her manner and voice, which, coupled with her extraordinary cleverness and assiduity, sometimes reminded me of the "Changeling" in Fairy Legends'.

Jane's intuition was only too horribly justified. Flo was found to be a hardened liar and a chronic mischief-maker.

'She began by bringing tales to her mistress of 'negligence and disagreeableness' on the part of the new cook, Mary, who had just replaced the unmourned mooncalf. At last, said Jane, 'my disatisfaction reached a climax, and I told this Mary that I perceived she would not suit'. 'The only person who looked delighted,' she adds, 'was Flo.'

But in a further interview with the tearful Mary, more horrors came to light. Flo had told Mary dreadful stories about Jane—gleaned, she alleged, from the departed Elizabeth of East Lothian.

Summoned by a shaking Jane, Flo tried to brazen it out. The scene which followed 'struck me deadly sick at stomach,' said Jane. '"If you please Ma'am," said Flo, "Elizabeth said a woman that was her fellow-servant in Scotland told her before she came here that you were a she-devil! and Elizabeth said *that* tall chair (pointing to a *prie-Dieu*) was for strapping you to when you were mad!!!"'

For once Jane's sense of humour deserted her utterly. There was something sinister, something viperish about Flo; she felt sick and stunned.

Mary now turned upon Flo. 'O, you lying bad girl! I see it all now; that you were set on driving me out of the place; and I shouldn't wonder if you did the same by Elizabeth.'

'The same thought,' said Jane, 'had just flashed on myself.' She remembered that from the day of Flo's arrival Elizabeth changed 'from a mere obedient blockhead into a sullen, disobliging blockhead, seeming rather to take pleasure in poisoning Mr. C. than not!'

At this point 'the imp', as Jane called her, seeing herself unmasked, began to cry very hard. ' "You will never bear me again, I know! I have been so *treacherous*! You were so kind to me; and I was fond of you! And I have been so very treacherous, ooh—ooh—oo-oh."'

'I didn't know what on earth to do,' said Jane.

But after another scene with Flo's mother, who tried to shift the blame on to Mary, Jane knew only too well what to do.

'The sooner you go the better—today if you like,' she told Flo. 'And in one hour she was gone!'

But the Changeling quickly recovered. 'Three days after she came over, tears all dried, looking hard and cold, to ask me to "see a Lady" for her. "What sort of a character do you think I can give you?" I asked. 'Well,' said the little child, "I have *told a few lies* and I have been *treacherous*; but that is all you can say against me!"'

'The dreadful child!' Jane exclaimed, and demanded of Mary Russell, 'Now do you wonder I feel ill?'

No wonder either that little Charlotte's peace-offering of violets was received so gladly; or that Jane was soon writing, 'I wish you had never left my house, Dear!' and suggesting that perhaps one day Charlotte might grow tired of 'bettering herself' and 'come back to me to be housemaid, and *valet* and *lady's maid*, and *friend* and *little Daughter. . . .*'

The vindicated Mary stayed on, and when Jane came home after her serious illness in 1864, she was one of the two maids who ran out into the street to greet her 'with flushed faces and tears in their eyes'. Mary, indeed, 'threw her arms round my neck and fell to kissing me in the open street!'

But Jane seemed destined to disillusionment. Only a few weeks later she began to make disturbing discoveries: the household accounts showed unheard-of extravagance—three pounds of butter eaten every week in the kitchen, half a pound of tea finished in four days. The linen was neglected and in rags, her best table-napkins had disappeared, and so had most of the china. The maids, questioned, were silent and sullen, and she decided to dismiss the housemaid, Helen.

Poor Jane! Yet another 'moral shock' was to come. This time it was administered by Mrs. Southam, Charlotte's aunt, normally 'a silent woman, never meddling'. What she had to tell, she said, was 'known to all the neighbours round here . . . and if I don't tell you now, you will blame me for having let you be so deceived'. 'Mary,' she continued, 'is the worst of girls. She had an illegitimate child in your house on the 29th of last July. It was her *second* child—and all the things you have been missing have been spent on her man and her friends. There has been constant company kept in your kitchen since there was no fear of *your* seeing it. . . .'

Jane could not believe her ears. Mary! Who had waited upon her in her illness, and gone with her as lady's maid to St. Leonards. 'If you had seen the creature,' she wrote to Mary Russell, 'you would as soon have suspected the Virgin Mary of such things!' But in her horror and disgust, Jane found a certain wry humour in the thought of Mr. Carlyle and Geraldine Jewsbury sitting talking in the dining-room while Mary was giving birth in the china closet—with 'just a thin small door between!'

On 15 November 1864, Mrs. Warren, a respectable widow of 50, arrived on the scene. Jane was taking no more chances with pairs of young girls. A 'young person'—Fanny II—was engaged as house-maid and lady's maid. She was, said Jane, 'modest and intelligent and, I should say from her face, not only honest but honourable'. There were to be no more illegitimate children.

Alas, we soon learn that Fanny is 'not agreeable—cries and sulks'. But with Mrs. Warren as housekeeper and cook, peace had at last descended over the Cheyne Row household: meals were punctual and wholesome; there were no complaints from Mr. C. Mrs. Warren did the shopping, and hampers of farm produce arrived every week from Addiscombe, as well as the usual offerings from Scotland.

Jane's health benefited. 'My appetite,' she said, 'has improved since I had the new cook, who makes everything *look* nice, however it may taste; and who regulates my dinners according to "her own sweet will".' She had herself weighed at the greengrocers—'swung up in the air like a basket of potatoes', and found that her weight was eight stones nine pounds—'fair enough for a woman of my inches'.

But Fanny had to go. 'My lady's maid has put me in a rage at least once every day'; and in May 1865 Jane wrote to Jessie Hiddle-stone, the daughter of an old family servant, offering her the place. 'What my housemaid has to do,' she said, 'is . . . to do the housework, to answer the door, to wait at table, to be the least bit of a lady's maid to me, and the least bit of a valet to Mr. Carlyle.' 'The work is not heavy,' she quickly adds, 'for anyone who under-stands her business. The Washing is all given out; only the servants wash their own clothes—there is a little garden to dry them in.'

Two months after the arrival of Mrs. Warren, Carlyle wrote the last word of the last volume of *Frederick the Great*. The attic ceased to be his study; he moved his desk and his books and pictures downstairs, and for the first time the basement kitchen became simply a kitchen, and the maids slept at the top of the house.

Jane was to enjoy a year of comparative tranquillity. At Christmas 1865 she sent little Charlotte a book, and wrote, 'Mrs. Warren continues to be a great comfort to me . . . the House goes on without any bother to me, and at no greater expense than when I did half the work myself, and had to teach the other half! But with all her cleverness, and nice looks, I have none of the *love* for Jessy I had for *you*: No servant has ever been for me the sort of *adopted child* that *you* were!'

By this time, Charlotte was engaged to be married, to Mr. Mills, a carpenter who lodged with her aunt in Lawrence Street; she was going to give up service when she married. But a stronger barrier than marriage was to come between Jane and her 'little daughter'.

In April 1866 Charlotte received a letter from Cheyne Row—but in a strange hand. It was from Geraldine Jewsbury.

'Dear Charlotte,' she wrote, 'This little bit of paper is large enough to hold the heavy tidings I have to tell you. Mrs. Carlyle is dead—she died yesterday quite suddenly while out driving— Dr. Quain says it was paralysis. Mr. Carlyle is not at home but he may come back tomorrow—it will be a terrible coming home for him. She was in her usual health and spirits and we none of us dreamed of danger.'

Jane's servant troubles—and who shall say they were not serious?—were over. She was brought home and laid upon her bed— 'my own red bed—that bed that I was born in'—and there Carlyle found her on his return.

Two candles burned beside her: the candles which, so many years before, she had seized from her mother before the soirée, and thrust into a cupboard. Mrs. Warren told Geraldine that one night when Jane was feeling ill 'she said to her, that when the last had come, she was to go upstairs into the closet of the spare room and there she would find two wax candles wrapt in paper, and that those were to be lighted and burned'.

'We found them and lighted them, and did as she desired', wrote Geraldine.

'Light is one of the things I do not like to economise in, when I am alone; just the more I am alone, the more light I need.' So Jane wrote to her husband in 1843, and perhaps he remembered now. It was he who would be alone in the dark old house, and all the lamps and candles in the world would not lessen his loneliness.

\*     \*     \*

The two good servants, Mrs. Warren and Jessie, stayed on, and the household ran smoothly on the lines laid down by its mistress. Materially, nothing was altered: Mr. C.'s kind of soup, Mr. C.'s cutlets, his bread-puddings, his bowl of porridge, were carefully made and served up at regular hours. He continued to complain, mildly, of indigestion to his brothers and sisters.

There were no more earthquakes; there were no scenes or dramas. The house was very quiet. In the drawing-room, Jane's piano stood closed and silent. Carlyle remembered the last time she had played it, only a week or two before her death.

'We two had come up from dinner and were sitting in this room . . . "Lie on the sofa there," said she . . . In old years I used to lie that way, and she would play the piano to me: a long series of Scotch tunes which set my mind finely wandering through the realms of memory and romance. . . . That evening I had lain but a few minutes when she turned round to her piano, got out the Thomson Burns book, and to my surprise and joy, broke out again into her bright little stream of harmony, . . . silent for at least ten years before, and gave me . . . all my old favourites.' 'That piano has never again sounded,' he added, 'nor in my time will or shall.'

Two years after Jane's death Carlyle's niece Mary Aitken came to Cheyne Row, to be companion and amanuensis to her uncle. For a young girl it cannot have been an easy task, and it speaks well for Mary's character that she remained with Carlyle for the rest of his life. 'She is a wise little thing,' he wrote in 1870, '*honest* I think as spring-water; pretty to look upon; and shines like a small taper, slightly breaking the gloom of this my new element.'

The house, Carlyle noticed in 1873, was 'all as clean as new pins'; and no doubt under Mary's careful eye nothing was allowed to grow shabby or dirty. But somehow, with Jane's death, the house ceased to be of importance: it was a shell, a covering for the great man. He was seen emerging from it for his daily walk along the river or his daily drive; being fetched in a nobleman's carriage to dine and be lionized; on Sundays going with Mary by omnibus to St. Paul's, where he enjoyed the organ music.

Mary did not attempt to alter the ways of the house. Jane's memory remained in the chintzes and damasks that she had sewn and dyed and mended, in the carpets that she had fitted and nailed down, grumbling at the damage to her hands; in the plain old-fashioned furniture that she had urged little Charlotte to keep clean and shining.

But things began to wear out. In 1874, Mary made a timid attempt to move with the times, and changed the colour scheme in the library. Jane's wall-paper with its pattern of large pink roses was replaced by one with a neat leafy design in dark green; the crimson curtains were dyed 'a pretty brown'. The dignified lines of the old Scottish furniture remained unspoilt; but Jane's elaborately patterned tablecloths and early Victorian chintzes were swept away, superseded by the fashionable, artistic, olive-green serge.

In his old age Carlyle used this room more and more. All his favourite books and pictures and pieces of furniture gradually congregated here. The screen which Jane had made for him in 1849 was brought up from the dining-room. . . . 'I have been busy', wrote Jane, 'off and on, for a great many months in pasting a screen . . . all over with prints. It will be a charming "work of art" when finished. . . .' In his new leather arm-chair—a present from John Forster—Carlyle sat day after day, reading, pondering, dozing, in the room which had seen so much of his own history and Jane's. It was here that he had struggled over *The French Revolution*—'an accursed *Punch* is shrieking under my windows!' he had written angrily in 1835: 'the curtains keep out squalid sights; but how exclude distractive sounds?' Here it was that Jane and he were sitting when Mill rushed in, pale and wild-eyed, with the news of the burnt manuscript. It was here that Jane had received her *émigrés*—Cavaignac, Mazzini, Pepoli and the rest; here where Dickens and d'Orsay, Tennyson, Browning ('I like Browning less

and less,' said Jane; 'and even *she* does not grow on me.'), Thackeray,
Ruskin, Darwin, had sat drinking tea and nibbling biscuits; here
where there had been so much good talk, such exchange of 'wits'—
such explosive intolerance of fools and humbugs.

It was here too that Jane sat alone with him in the evenings,
enlivening him, while he lay and smoked, with her pithy anecdotes
about small daily events, her imitations of Helen that were 'among
the most amusing things I ever heard'.

Towards the end of Carlyle's life there were three important
changes. In 1877 the house ceased to be number 5 and became
number 24 Cheyne Row; Mary Aitken married her cousin Alexander
Carlyle; and in the course of time the old spare room upstairs
became the nursery, and infant cries were heard in the house. By
this time Carlyle lived entirely on the first floor, sleeping in Jane's
bedroom and walking through the connecting doors into his library.

The final change came early in 1881. His new brass bedstead was
moved into the library; and on 5 February, at half past eight in the
morning, the new holland blinds were pulled down over the
windows. Thomas Carlyle was dead.

The house where, for 126 years before the Carlyles came,
people had lived, been born, and died, and where Carlyle had lived
for forty-seven years, now ceased to be a home. In 1895 it became,
officially, a Memorial.

But houses depend, for their character, upon people. Number 24
Cheyne Row, is a house with a very strong character.

THE END

24 Cheyne Row
5 February 1964

# APPENDIX

## THE SERVANTS AT CHEYNE ROW DURING MRS. CARLYLE'S LIFETIME

1834, June

BESSY BARNET, from Warwickshire. 'By far the orderliest, cleverest worker we have ever had in the house . . . and has manners and an appearance of character totally beyond the servant class.' (T.C. to his mother, June 1834.)
Bessy was obliged to leave after a few months, for family reasons.

?December

JANE IRELAND, from Lancaster. 'Very amiable, intelligent, and much liked here, tho' hopelessly incompetent, and obliged to be sent home. One day, at breakfast time, she was found sitting by the unlighted, half-scoured grate, sunk overhead in Goethe's *Wilhelm Meister*. . . .' (T.C. in *New Letters and Memorials*.)

1835, June–July

IRISH PROTESTANT, nameless. 'The best servant I ever had, tho' a rather unamiable person in temper. . . .' (J.W.C. to Mrs. Aitken.) Suddenly sent for 'to attend a sick mother', and Jane made do for three or four weeks with a charwoman 'who has her family in the workhouse'.

August–September

IRISH CATHOLIC, also nameless. 'Active, tidy-looking', but bad tempered. 'Our Irish Catholic maid proved a mutinous Irish savage—had a fixed persuasion, I could notice, that our poor house, and we, had been made for *her*, and had gone awry in the process. One evening . . . was instantly dismissed by me—"To your room at once; wages tomorrow morning; disappear!".' (T.C. in *Letters and Memorials*.)

October

SARAH HEATHER ('Sereetha the Peesweep'). 'A very feeble though willing little girl.' (T.C. in *Letters and Memorials*.)

End of October     ANNE COOK, from Annandale. 'Hardy as a High-lander, full of assiduity, good-nature, and wild Annandale savagery, which causes the Cockney mind here to pause astonished. Broader Scotch was never spoken or thought by any mortal in this Metropolitan city.' (T.C. to his mother, December 1835.) July 1837, sent back to Annan in disgrace. 'God help her, for her case is beyond the reach of mortal help.' (J.W.C. to T.C., 17 July 1837.)

1837, July     ELLEN. 'A sweet girl—does her very best to please.' (J.W.C. to T.C., July 1837.)

?December     HELEN MITCHELL, from Kirkcaldy. 'We have never had *so comfortable a bit useful* creature about the house.' (T.C., 1840.) '. . . In a sense, the only servant we ever got to belong to us, and be one of our household, in this place.' (T.C. in *Letters and Memorials.*)

1844, May–June     MARIA, who came during Helen's holiday and left in Mid-June when Helen returned. 'Poor Maria! she had been *crying* off and on for the last two days—certainly I have a wonderful luck for in-spiring fervent *passions* to servant-maids!' (J.W.C. to Babbie Welsh, June 1844.)

1846, end of November     HELEN leaves, to housekeep for her brother, a manufacturer of coach-fringe, in Dublin.
ISABELLA arrives. 'She had been carefully trained by pious Edinburgh ladies; was filled with con-sciousness of free grace, and, I believe, would have got more education, as I told her, if she had been left to puddle through the gutters with her neglected fellow brats.' (T.C. in *Letters and Memorials.*) Nicknamed 'Pessima'; left declaring that no woman living could do the work expected of her by the Carlyles.

1846, mid-December     'OLD HALF DEAD COOK', nameless, 'whom a lady who was going to part with her at any rate, on account of her "shocking bad temper", obligingly made over to us . . . at an hour's notice'. (J.W.C. to Mrs. Stirling, December 1846.)

31 December     ANNE II, 'a cheery little button of a creature, with a sort of cockney resemblance to Helen'. (T.C. in

*Letters and Memorials*.) 'I think I am even strong enough in Anne's respect to even smoke in her presence.' (J.W.C. to T.C., October 1847.) 1848, autumn, Anne II leaves to be married to butcher's assistant; they go and live in Jersey.

1848, autumn HELEN, who has quarrelled with her brother, returns.

1849, February HELEN discovered 'mortal drunk'. Final dismissal of Helen.

ELIZABETH SPRAGUE, from Exeter. 'She is far the most loveable servant I ever had. . . . My only fear about her is that being only four-and-twenty, and calculated to produce an impression on the other sex, she may weary of single service.' (J.W.C. to Mrs. Aitken.)

1850, August 'That dreadful Elizabeth' left, after a series of scenes. Followed by ELIZA, 'a little girl who had never been out before, who could not cook a morsel of food or make a bed, or do any civilised thing without having me at her heels.' (J.W.C. to T.C., August 1850.)

29 August EMMA, from Essex. 'Not what is called a *thorough* servant, but that will be no objection to signify, as I am not a thorough lady.' (J.W.C. to T.C., 2 September 1850.) 'Mutton broth is beyond her, and in roasting, she is far from strong.' (J.W.C. to T.C., 23 September 1850.) End of September, Emma dismissed.

December 'I have been . . . bothered to death with servants this autumn—have had three in quick succession.' (J.W.C. to Mary Russell, 31 December 1850.)

to 'The first (EMMA) roasted fowls with the crop and bowels in them.'

'The second, a really clever servant and good girl, came to me with a serious disease upon her, and had to be sent to hospital. . .' (This was probably FANNY, who returned later—see IRISH FANNY.)

1851, January 'The third and last, thank Heaven, suits capitally —but I had best not praise her too much, it is a "tempting of Providence". . . .'

| | |
|---|---|
| | It was, for this nameless servant went deaf on New Year's Day, 1851. At the end of February she gave notice, declaring that she would 'certainly die of grief if she went on listening to bells and never hearing them'. |
| March | 'I suppose I shall get hardened to changes like other people. . . .' (J.W.C. to Babbie Welsh, March 1851.) |
| 31 March | Nameless servant. 'Less *sensitive* looking but more *sentimental*. . . . Has a three years' character and can cook—especially *fish*. . . .' |
| 11 May | 'Oh horror! the old story of a change of servants to be gone over again the week after next!' (J.W.C. to Babbie.) |
| 31 May | ANN III—'a thoroughly good, respectable woman —the best *character* I ever had in the house.' (J.W.C. to Helen Welsh.) 'I hope she will stay— forever—if that were possible.' (J.W.C. to Mary Russell, January 1852.) |
| 1852, May–June | ANN gets ill. LITTLE MARTHA engaged temporarily. 'The dearest little girl of fifteen . . . she reads beautifully and writes beautifully and *sews* beautifully—has the most soothing manners, and the most upright disposition.' (J.W.C. to Kate Sterling, July 1852.) |
| 1852, ?July | ANN appears to have made a brief reappearance, for in July Jane wrote to Babbie Welsh: 'Ann is much more effective and obliging than for long before she went away and will do quite well "until we go to Germany". Especially as I know of an adorable cook to assist whenever I want her.' However, by mid-July, Ann, unable, perhaps, to face a household earthquake, disappeared. |
| Mid-July | Nameless servant known as THE BEAUTY, 'engaged because (Carlyle) decidedly liked her physiognomy.' (J.W.C. to Dr. Carlyle.) 'Our Beauty was as perfect a fool as the sun ever shone on, and at the end of a week *left*, finding it "quite impossible to live in any such muddle".' (J.W.C. to T.C., 3 August 1852.) |
| | LITTLE MARTHA asked to remain till the end of |

August. 'Little Martha is gone to bed the happiest child in Chelsea at the honour done her.' (J.W.C. to T.C.)

End of August    IRISH FANNY comes back. 'The best comfort I ever had.' 'Really a nice servant; a dash of Irish "rough and ready" in her, but a good cleaner, and a good cook, and a perfect incarnation of "the Willing Mind!"' (J.W.C. to T.C., September 1852.)

1853, July    'Mr. C. *exploded* Fanny some fortnight ago—and I was vexed with him at the time, for my natural cowardice inclined me to *puddle on* with Irish-cabinism and a *"cloud of lies"* rather than front the horrors of change . . . but now that the creature is fairly gone . . . I am glad.' (J.W.C. to Kate Sterling, July 1853.)

'I have the old cook who was with me last year till I am suited.' (Ibid.) (This was almost certainly MRS. NEWNHAM, who lived nearby, the 'adorable cook' referred to above.)

August    ANN III returns; stays nearly five years.

1858, February    'That unblessed Ann . . . has caused me more irritation than she is worth. . . .' 'My affairs with Ann have become critical.' (J.W.C. to Mary Russell.)

29 March    'Ann left at midday.' (J.W.C. to Mary Russell.)

MISS CAMERON, from Inverness. 'Daughter of a half-pay Lieutenant.' 'Having never filled but *one* situation, that of Lady's-maid and Companion . . . does not know, naturally, whether she can clean a house, and cook a dinner, till she have tried!!! Hopes that she will soon learn. . . .' (J.W.C. to M.R.)

15 April    Miss Cameron convicted of lying and theft, and ran out of the house late at night, never to be seen again.

There is a hiatus here. Mrs. Carlyle must have made do with local help, possibly LITTLE MARTHA or MRS. NEWNHAM, till June.

June    CHARLOTTE SOUTHAM ('Little Charlotte'). 'A fine little Chelsea creature—courageously, with excellent discernment, and with very good success,

now taken on trial.' (T.C. in *Letters and Memorials*.)
'My young maid is a jewel of a creature.' (J.W.C.
to M.R., 27 June.)

1860, August      Charlotte 'needing to be put under some *stricter*
superintendence than mine. . . . I gave her
warning and engaged a so-called "Treasure" in
her stead.' (J.W.C. to M.R., October 1860.)

1860, August      OLD JANE, aged 71, engaged. Asks for 'a pair of
young legs' to assist her.

SARAH, aged 16, told to come in September.

End of August      Old Jane 'a perfectly incompetent cook and
servant'. (J.W.C. to T.C.) 'Finished off by stealing
eight bottles of ale.' (J.W.C. to M.R.)
Little Charlotte comes in to nurse Jane, who re-
sists the temptation to take her back.

September      TALL CHARLOTTE (housemaid), engaged to be
'head' to Sarah (cook). 'So now I am mistress of
*two* servants—and ready to hang myself!' (J.W.C.
to M.R., October 1860.)

November      'Tall Charlotte' given notice; LITTLE CHARLOTTE
reinstated. 'I have had a great fret taken off me, in
the removal of that vulgar, conceited woman, and
the restoration of little Charlotte. . . .' 'It is a
curious establishment with something of the sound
and character of a nursery. Charlotte not nineteen
till next March, and Sarah seventeen last week.'
(J.W.C. to Maggie Welsh, December 1860.)

1861, June      SARAH went away, ill.

CHARLOTTE left, to better herself.

MATILDA (cook).

MARGARET (housemaid), 'a little, black, busy
creature'. (T.C. in *Letters and Memorials*.)

July      Matilda rushed to St. George's Hospital, with a
strangulated hernia.

ELIZABETH, from East Lothian, comes as cook.

1862 ? Summer      MARGARET leaves; is succeeded by MARIA.

October      Maria is not a success with Jane. 'My fine lady
housemaid.' 'I have foreseen for long, even when
she was capering about me, and kissing my hands
and shawl, that this emotional young lady would
not wear well.'

1862, November · MARIA leaves, under protest.

Elizabeth II is a disastrous failure. 'My Scotch blockhead.' 'Such a woman to have had sent four hundred miles to one! Mr. C. always speaks of her as "that horse", "that cow", "that mooncalf"! But upon my honour, it is an injustice to the horse, the cow, and even the mooncalf.' (J.W.C. to Mary Russell.) Maria is replaced by FLO. 'A remarkably intelligent, well-conditioned girl between fourteen and fifteen, who was christened "Florence"—too long and too romantic a name for household use!' Flo 'is extremely intelligent, active and willing'.

End of November · ELIZABETH sent back to East Lothian, after 'driving Mr. C. out of his senses with her block-headisms'.

MARY engaged as cook: 'a girl of twenty-four with an excellent three years' character'. (J.W.C. to Mrs. Braid, December 1862.)

1863, January · Flo discovered to be 'an incomparable small demon' and dismissed for slander and lying.

LIZZY engaged as kitchen-maid.

Mary acts as housemaid and lady's maid.

'Jolly, clever, elderly woman' (MRS. NEWNHAM?) comes in, temporarily, to cook. 'I almost wish the present arrangement, tho' an expensive one, could last. . . .' (J.W.C. to M.R., January 1863.)

May · 'My present pair of girls go on very peaceably. They are neither of them particularly bright.' (J.W.C. to Betty Braid, May 1863.)

1863, autumn · HELEN II engaged as housemaid.

Mary remains as cook and lady's maid.

These two servants were in the house during the long illness after Jane's street accident. 'My servants have been most kind and unwearied in their attentions.' (J.W.C. to M.R.)

1864, October · On Jane's return to Cheyne Row the maids came out to meet her 'looking *timidly*, with flushed faces, and tears in their eyes! And the little one (the cook) threw her arms round my neck and fell to kissing me in the open street; and the big one (the housemaid) I had to kiss, that she might not be made *jealous,* the first thing!' (J.W.C. to M.R., October 1864.)

**November**

After discovering signs of waste, breakages and mysterious disappearance of much of her linen, Jane 'got a moral shock which would, I think, have *killed* me at St. Leonard's' (i.e. during her illness). Mary had given birth to an illegitimate child the previous July, which, with Helen's help, had been smuggled out of the house.

Mary and Helen both dismissed.

**November**

MRS. WARREN engaged as cook-housekeeper. '. . . a respectable widow of fifty. . . . If she only go on as she has begun, I shall say I have lighted on "a treasure"—at last!' (J.W.C. to Anne Welsh, 30 November.)

FANNY II engaged as housemaid and lady's maid. 'The young person (eight and twenty) who came for housemaid and lady's maid also promises excellently.' (Ibid.) 'It is a real blessing to have got good efficient, comfortable servants at last, and I may say I have earned it by the amount of bad servants I have endured.' (J.W.C. to Mrs. Austin, February 1865.)

**1865, March**

'My . . . only discontents have been from my Lady's Maid, who has put me in a rage at least once every day.' (J.W.C. to Mrs. Oliphant.)

**15 May**

Mrs. Carlyle writes to JESSIE HIDDLESTONE, daughter of her mother's old servant, offering her the post of housemaid. 'Jessie Hiddlestone is in Thornhill, awaiting my orders—the most promising-looking servant we have had since her mother. I am greatly pleased with her . . .' (J.W.C. to T.C., from Scotland, 28 June 1865.)

**December**

'Jessie, the Thornhill girl, is going on quite satisfactorily, since I ceased treating her too kindly . . .' (J.W.C. to Mrs. Austin.)

**1866, January**

'I have got Jessie pretty well in hand now. It is mortifying, after all my romantic hopes of her, to find that kindness goes for nothing with her, and that she is only amenable to good sharp snubbing. Well, she shall have it! At the same time, I make

a point of being just to her and being kind to her, as a *mistress* to a *servant*. So she got the "nice dress" at Christmas, along with Mrs. Warren; but I put no affection into anything I do for her, and let her see that I don't. It was a lucky Christmas for her. Mr. Ruskin always gives my servants a sovereign apiece at that season. "The like had never happened to her before", she was obliged to confess. She went to the theatre one night with some Fergussons, and has acquaintances enough. So I hope she is happy, though I don't like her.'
(J.W.C. to Mary Russell, 29 January 1866.)

# NOTE ON SOURCES

The information contained in this book has been gathered from the following sources:—

REMINISCENCES BY THOMAS CARLYLE, edited by J. A. Froude (Longmans, Green & Co., 1881).

LETTERS OF THOMAS CARLYLE, edited by C. E. Norton (Macmillan, 1886).

LETTERS OF THOMAS CARLYLE TO HIS YOUNGEST SISTER, edited by Charles Townsend Copeland (Chapman & Hall, 1899).

NEW LETTERS OF THOMAS CARLYLE, edited by Alexander Carlyle (John Lane, the Bodley Head, 1904).

THOMAS CARLYLE: A HISTORY OF HIS LIFE IN LONDON, by James Anthony Froude, M.A. (Longmans, Green & Co., 1885).

LETTERS AND MEMORIALS OF JANE WELSH CARLYLE, edited by J. A. Froude (Longmans, Green & Co., 1883).

NEW LETTERS AND MEMORIALS OF JANE WELSH CARLYLE, annotated by Thomas Carlyle and edited by Alexander Carlyle (John Lane, the Bodley Head, 1903).

JANE WELSH CARLYLE: LETTERS TO HER FAMILY, edited by Leonard Huxley, LL.D. (John Murray, 1924).

EARLY LETTERS OF JANE WELSH CARLYLE, edited by D. G. Ritchie (Longmans, Green & Co., 1889).

JANE WELSH AND JANE CARLYLE, by Elizabeth Drew (Harcourt Brace & Company, Inc., 1928).

THE NECESSARY EVIL, by Lawrence and Elisabeth Hanson (Constable & Company, 1952).

JANE WELSH CARLYLE: Letters, selected by Trudy Bliss (Gollancz, 1950).

CHELSEA, by William Gaunt (Batsford, 1954).

CARLYLE'S HOUSE, CHELSEA, Illustrated Catalogue, Chronology and Descriptive Notes, by Alexander Carlyle (*Country Life*, Ltd., for the National Trust, 1954).

Unpublished letters from Jane Carlyle to Kate Sterling and Thomas Carlyle to Mrs. Wedgwood; part of a collection presented to Carlyle's House in 1962 by Arthur M. Woodward, grandson of Kate Sterling.

Unpublished letter from Jane Carlyle to Mr. Cross, Melchett Park, Romsey, Hants; given to the authoress by Mrs. E. F. Charlton in October 1962, and now the property of the National Trust.

# INDEX

Warren, Mrs. (servant), 180–2, 192–3
Washing and bathing facilities, 9, 48–9
Water supply, 11, 33, 49, 78, 147–8; rate, 142, 147
Wellington, Duke of, 79
Welsh, Grace (Jane's aunt), 139
Welsh, Mrs. Grace Baillie (Jane's mother), 42–3, 110–1, 128, 157–60; stays at Cheyne Row, 18–21, 23–5, 27; Jane's relations with, 20–1, 24–5, 27; taking of pills, 21, 42; soirée incident, 24–5, 181; Helen's liking for, 27–8; nettle from grave planted

in Cheyne Row garden, 159–60
Welsh, Helen, 76, 81, 109, 118, 135
Welsh, Jeannie (Babbie), 65, 69–70, 72–3, 107, 110, 116
Welsh, Walter, 158
Whinnyrigg, 24
White, Mrs. (servant), 38–9
White Falcon, Order of, 170–1
William IV, 19
Willis's Rooms, 23
Wilton Crescent, 131
Wimbledon, 47
Woolner, Thomas, 3–4
Wright, Mr., 165
'Wristikins', 104